HERBERT HOOVER

and

AMERICAN INDIVIDUALISM

THE MACMILLAN COMPANY
NEW YORK · BOSTON · CHICAGO · DALLAS
ATLANTA · SAN FRANCISCO

MACMILLAN & CO., Limited
LONDON · BOMBAY · CALCUTTA
MELBOURNE

THE MACMILLAN COMPANY
OF CANADA, Limited
TORONTO

HERBERT HOOVER
AND AMERICAN INDIVIDUALISM

A Modern Interpretation
of a National Ideal

By

WALTER FRIAR DEXTER
PRESIDENT OF WHITTIER COLLEGE

New York
THE MACMILLAN COMPANY
1932

TO

WILLIAM IRVING HOLLINGSWORTH

*whose personal appreciation of
President Hoover and his
principles of human progress
inspired the writing of this book.*

FOREWORD

HERBERT HOOVER is the leading modern American exponent of the philosophy of individualism. Spoken and written statements covering this phase of human interest, during the past decade, have won for him the intellectual approbation of many of the best thinkers of the civilized world. His confidence in the ability of and his respect for the common man as set forth in his doctrine of individual expression, have created a spirit of personal and national loyalty enjoyed only by men whose high and noble purposes are determined by the needs and aspirations of the people whom they serve.

And yet his messages have been misunderstood and his policies misinterpreted by many who have been aroused to a point of sharp disagreement primarily because of the habits of collective action to which they became accustomed during the War. This social controversy, nation wide in scope, has brought this subject into the forum of public discussion and has made it worthy of study and investigation. Accordingly the title of this book requires an analysis of the President's theory of human progress and it allows the author and his readers a mental excursion into this field of human relations, limited only by the implications involved. Mr.

Hoover's name does not appear in every paragraph, nor even on every page, but his experience and philosophy furnish the structural framework of the entire book.

The philosophic principles contained in these pages could not have been assembled except for the generous permission granted by Doubleday, Doran and Company to quote freely from the little book, "American Individualism," written by Herbert Hoover in 1923.

CONTENTS

CHAPTER I

Born in Iowa—of Quaker Stock

Hoover an Individualist. The Iowa Country and
Its People. Local Environment. The West Branch
Free School. Membership in the Religious Society
of Friends. Social Service in Society of Friends.
Economic Inheritance. Western Contacts. The
Presidential Challenge.

"I am proud to have been born in Iowa."

"It was settled by the adventurous, the courageous, who fought their way across the ever-extending frontier; they have builded here in so short a period as seventy-five years a state with the least poverty, the highest average intelligence, the most generous education which ever blessed a single commonwealth."

"I come of Quaker stock."

H. H.

CHAPTER I

Born in Iowa—of Quaker Stock

HOOVER AN INDIVIDUALIST

To have been born in Iowa and to have come of Quaker stock are reasons, sufficient in themselves, to cause President Hoover to be an ardent American Individualist. His environmental and religious background gave sanction and support to this theory of life which was to be strengthened and more definitely formulated through his contact in later years with people living under wide and varied social and governmental conditions. Since the World War, both his thoughts and his emotions have undergone the searching analysis of reason and research. He now favors without equivocation or compromise the doctrine of American Individualism.

With considerable confidence he explains his position without leaving his hearer in doubt as to his point of view upon this important American ideal:

"For myself, let me say at the very outset that my faith in the essential truth, strength, and vitality of the developing creed by which we have hitherto lived in this country of ours has been confirmed and deepened by the searching experiences of seven years of service in the backwash and misery of war. Seven years of contending with economic degenera-

3

tion, with social disintegration, with incessant political dislocation, with all of its seething and ferment of indivioual and class conflict, could but impress me with the primary motivation of social forces, and the necessity for broader thought upon their great issues to humanity. And from it all I emerge an individualist—an unashamed individualist. But let me say also that I am an American individualist. For America has been steadily developing the ideals that constitute progressive individualism."

In order to understand Mr. Hoover's individualistic philosophy we must attempt to gain some insight into the causes of his emotional attitude. We must know why he feels as well as thinks in terms of individualism. We must study his early environment and his religion—the former because of the general impression it made and the latter because of the motives it shaped and released.

His early childhood environment favored the formation of an individualistic philosophy of life, not only because it stimulated thought along this line but because it created a feeling of the fitness of such an ideal. Accordingly his idea concerning this fundamental human problem is more than a theory; it is a conviction.

THE IOWA COUNTRY AND ITS PEOPLE

The fifty years preceding the date of his birth was a period of extraordinary importance in the development of the state of Iowa. At the beginning of this period it was an open territory with seemingly unlimited agricultural possibilities. The soil was rich and deep; water was plentiful and almost universally distributed. Timber and mineral resources were easily accessible for the ordinary mechanical and industrial needs of the time. Such physical and topographical conditions once they were properly advertised, stimulated the pioneer homeseekers to take up homesteads and build permanent dwellings to an extent perhaps unequaled in the westward movement of the American people. The great Black Hawk territory rapidly assumed the characteristics and proportions of a state. Iowa had the distinct advantage, lying as it does, just west of the Mississippi River and north of the big plantation area, of becoming a community of progress and advancement, unhampered by traditions and customs which often fastened themselves on other sections of the United States. This state served as a meeting place for the former residents of the New England, the Middle Atlantic, and the South Atlantic states, and the children and grandchildren of the pioneers who had moved westward at an earlier time into the territory immediately east of the Mississippi River. All of these folk brought their own manners and methods of life. Religious, educational and governmental principles which had grown out of their experiences in the older states were given opportunity in this new territory to fuse into a system of new ideals and practices.

Just as this socializing process was taking place

groups of people began to arrive from England, France, and Germany. In England associations had been organized for the purpose of encouraging and directing emigrants to the new and promising territory. The pioneer builders would sometimes return to their mother country in order to give information relative to the opportunities in the new West. Mr. J. B. Newhall who had lived in Iowa for a period of ten years published a hand book for British emigrants in 1844 in which he gave the following instructions: "If the emigrants intend settling in Iowa, Southern Illinois, or Missouri: I would advise them to go by the way of New Orleans; the expense is much less, and there are fewer difficulties to contend with than in any other route. On their arrival in New Orleans, they can leave their families on board the ship, until they have made choice of a steamboat to convey them up the Mississippi; this can be accomplished in a few hours. The distance from the ship landing to the steamboat landing is little more than a mile. By going by way of New Orleans, they will be better able to take more heavy luggage. No charge will be made by the ship or steamboat for luggage. Families leaving this country ought to start not later than the latter part of March."

Towns and villages were named after cities in England and schools and churches similar to those with which they were familiar were founded.

While no permanent colonies nor towns seem to have been established during this early period by the French immigrants, their indirect influence was important and far-reaching. By following the leadership of such men as Jacques Marquette, Louis Joliet and Cavalier de la Salle they left their religious and intellectual impress upon the Commonwealth.

By far the largest number of people who came from Europe to the Black Hawk territory was of German origin. These traveled in groups numbering from a few persons to as many as two hundred and fifty. There are within the state today some four hundred thousand Germans and their descendants. This is approximately one-sixth of the entire population. Germany now furnishes more than one-third of the entire foreign-born population of the state.

These three groups coming as they did in large numbers from the Northern part of Europe, brought with them their financial resources, their social and economic customs and their spiritual ideals. While these did not in all instances fuse with the customs and conventionalities brought by the immigrants from the eastern states, nevertheless a great human interaction resulted.

In the decade between 1850 and 1860 nearly five hundred thousand people came into Iowa. Perhaps the most notable immigration took place between 1854 and 1856 when approximately two hundred thousand homeseekers arrived. In describing this overland movement an eye witness says:

"The immigration into Iowa the present season

(1854) is astonishing and unprecedented. For miles and miles, day after day, the prairies of Illinois are lined with cattle and wagons, pushing on towards this prosperous State. At a point beyond Peoria, during a single month, seventeen hundred and forty-three wagons had passed, and all for Iowa."

Here a new civilization arose. Through individual initiative and enterprise the vast domain of public land rapidly became private farms under the management of men who for the most part could not be charged, as we have seen and shall see later, with the sole ambition of private financial gain. They, like their forefathers, were seeking a land of economic, political, intellectual, and spiritual freedom.

Iowa was the first free state west of the Mississippi River. It became a place of ordered freedom, private initiative, equity of opportunity, and mutual service. It was not the birthplace of American Individualism but it was here that the ideal reached its highest level of expression. The early residents of this territory naturally became individualists. Their environment was conducive to the development of such a philosophy. Pioneers usually are individualists. Rarely, however, are they selfish individualists because selfish people need to be in a position to enjoy the fruits of their neighbors' work without an expenditure of too much effort on their own part. This they could not do with any degree of success on the prairies of Iowa. Life on the frontier required honesty, simplicity, frugality and withal a spirit of mutual helpfulness. Iowa individualism became a democratic individualism of the highest character. It was the outgrowth of a deep and abiding appreciation of the personal worth of an individual.

Into this free territory along with tens of thouands of other seekers of truth and freedom came the paternal great grandparents and the maternal grandparents of Herbert Hoover.

Jesse and Rebecca Hoover, together with their family, came to West Branch, in 1853, where they settled on a nearby farm. Eli, one of their sons and the father of three sons, Jesse, Allan, and Davis, engaged in farming one-half mile west of the village.

Theodore and Mary Minthorn, with two sons, John and Pennington, and five daughters, Anna, Huldah, Ellen Agnes, and Phoebe, having learned of the opportunities offered in this new and growing community decided to make this their future home. Having purchased three horses, they made the journey in a covered wagon from Toronto, Canada, their home, to Detroit, Michigan, where they entrained for Iowa. Not wanting to be separated, the family decided to ride in the caboose of the train which carried their possessions. They bought a farm two miles east and a mile south of West Branch. This was in 1860.

Ten years later, one morning in May, Huldah Minthorn, and Jesse Hoover walked to the Meeting House, which the Hoover family had helped to build, and were married according to the custom of the Society of Friends. Such a marriage furnished the democratic background of family life among the Friends, sometimes called Quakers. By virtue of the fact that the bride, in the presence of the assembled Friends who had previously expressed approval of the marriage, and who had arranged the meeting in which it was consummated, made exactly the same promise in becoming the wife as the groom used in becoming the husband, she was considered of equal importance and granted equal privilege and opportunity. He said, "In the presence of the Lord, and before this assembly, I take thee, Hulda Minthorn, to be my wife, promising with divine assistance to be unto thee a loving and faithful husband so long as we both shall live." She likewise said, "In the presence of the Lord and before this assembly I take thee, Jesse Hoover, to be my husband, promising with divine assistance to be unto thee a loving and faithful wife so long as we both shall live." Having entered into this simple but binding agreement they affixed their signatures to the wedding certificate which carried the names of all members present who cared to sign the document as witnesses. This certificate gave legal and spiritual sanction to the founding of an American home in which Herbert Hoover, the descendant of a long line of Quaker ancestors was born August 10, 1874.

LOCAL ENVIRONMENT

If in that year the people of America had been choosing a community as the birthplace of our president, they could have done no better than to have chosen West Branch, Iowa. The founders of the village could have had no thought of the distinction which would sometime belong to it because of the birth of a president within its limits. But be that as it may, the physical character of the territory lent itself to the building of a community which would naturally produce an individual with presidential possibilities.

The stage road between Iowa City and Davenport provided a main street through the town that was used by the people traveling between these larger centers of interest. It furnished not only the atmosphere of an ordinary main street of a western rural village, but the inspiration of a busy thoroughfare as well. On his way back and forth to the village school, Herbert Hoover crossed this public highway. The house in which he was born is located one block south on the west side of Downey Street on the north bank of the west branch of Wapsinonoc Creek, and the one in which he later lived is still farther south by one block on the opposite side of the street.

Picture, if you will then, a lad leaving his home in the south part of the village, passing his father's blacksmith shop, crossing the public highway, climbing the hill past the Quaker Meeting House to the public school which sat on the summit. A combination of organizations and institutions could not be more perfectly arranged as a setting for the development of a broad and civic outlook. American civilization as a whole was epitomized in this village.

The two-room house in which Herbert Hoover spent his early childhood was, and is, attractive in every detail. The little room, thirteen and one-half feet long and seven feet wide, in which he was born, looked out upon a yard and playground typically American. The living room which was used for a parlor, kitchen, and dining room combined, lent itself to the development of a superior social atmosphere. Parents and children together in such homes assumed the responsibility and enjoyed the privilege of collectively preparing the meals, entertaining the neighbors and carrying forward the routine activities of the household.

The farm upon which he lived after the death of his mother gave a wider but similar experience. "I do have a vivid recollection," said he, in speaking before the Iowa Society of Washington, D. C., in 1927, "that the major purpose of a farm was to produce a living right on the spot for the family. I know by experience that a family then produced all of its own vegetables, carried its grain to the nearest mill for grinding on toll, cut and hauled its own fuel from the wonderful woods ten miles away, and incidently gathered walnuts. The family wove its own carpets and some of its clothes, made its own soap, preserved its own meat and fruit and vegetables, got its sweetness from sorghum and honey. These families consumed perhaps eighty per cent of the product of their land. Twenty per cent of it was exchanged for the few outside essentials and to pay interest on the mortgage."

But Herbert Hoover's activities were limited neither by the territorial lines surrounding the home nor by the nature of the work to which he daily set his hand. He projected his personality into the recreational and play life of the neighborhood.

"There is no imprint upon our minds," says he, "so deep as those of early boyhood. Mine are the joys of Iowa—the glories of snowy winter, the wonder at the growing crops, the joining of the neighbors to harvest, the gathering of apples, the pilgrimage to the river woods for the annual fuel and nuts, the going to school, the interludes from work, in the swimming hole, fishing in creeks, the hunting for prairie chickens and rabbits in the hedges and woods. It is the entry to life which I could wish for every American boy and girl."

The problem of home-making with its program of work and recreation, was experienced as well as taught. The process had an individualizing effect upon the family group which in turn reacted upon the individual members.

Near the Hoover home stood the blacksmith shop in which the birth of a son was announced, and prophecy made that some day he would be president of the United States. Perhaps no type of work in the average Iowa community gave greater opportunity for social contact than did that of blacksmithing. To the blacksmith shop the farmers brought their plows and planters and other farm tools for sharpening and repair. The road builders came with their graders and scrapers and plows, the stage coach drivers with their wagons and harness and horses, the well diggers with their hoes and spades and drills, and the miners with their picks and crowbars and shovels. The woodsman brought his axe and wedge and saw. All of them came to visit.

As the tradesmen docked at the city of Tarsus in the days of Paul, so the community builders of Iowa visited the blacksmith shop of Jesse Clark Hoover. Not only did this vocation tend to emphasize and stress the necessity and importance of vocational and professional preparation, but it carried with it a socializing influence of strength and power. The activities of the home and of the vocation so far as the Hoover family was concerned, were intimately and vitally related by virtue of the proximity of the one to the other. Together they laid the foundation of a socialized conscience, which in turn paved the way for the school and the church to train in the high ideals of worthy citizenship.

THE WEST BRANCH FREE SCHOOL

From the doorstep of the school which Herbert Hoover attended he could survey the surrounding territory and see here and there the organizations and institutions that have made possible American civilization. In spite of the fury of the winter storms the Iowa pioneers established the custom of locating their schools on the most prominent points in their respective communities. Such a practice carries to this day the implication that this institution is the common meeting place of all local interests.

To have had the opportunity of attending an Iowa public school is an item of no small importance in the life of a man who is now charged with the responsibility of giving direction to American Democracy. It was here that his teacher Miss Molly Brown, introduced Herbert Hoover through the printed page to some of the problems of a larger social circumference. She had been appointed to the position which she then held because of her ability to create a respect for the high purpose of voluntary citizenship. This ability on her part was not only recognized by her school board but by the students whom she taught. They will tell you now that through the power of friendship and mutual understanding she was able to govern a class of boys and girls who up to the time of her employment had been considered beyond the realm of easy direction. The pupils were members of the second and third generations of Iowa pioneers. They had inherited the best of both the old and new world systems of instruction. It was here that public education really became a popular concern.

The schools of this period were conducted under the authority of the state school code which had been adopted in 1858. The broad principles which were written into this document owe their origin to the comprehensive knowledge of Horace Mann, who had spent a number of years in shaping the educational policies of the state of Massachusetts and who had traveled in Europe for the purpose of bringing to America reform measures which might prove beneficial to our school systems. Then too, he had, as president of Antioch College, an opportunity to observe many new educational measures in operation in the comparatively new state of Ohio. State authorities recognized the necessity of formulating an educational code in harmony with the intellectual and moral capacity of the populace whom they served. They knew that the relationship between law-making and educational progress was analogous to the relationship between railroad building and civilization. As the railroads, which were the results of civilization within populated and socialized areas, became the instruments of advancement on the western frontier, so the educational laws which were the product of a well-established civilization in the older parts of the continent and in Europe, became the instruments of educational advancement in America.

The citizens of this great state in the center of a mighty nation adopted four foundation principles upon which to build a system of education which they believed would be successfully directed by teachers of moral and intellectual power. The people wanted every youth in the state to have an education in "the elements of knowledge." They made it a separate and distinct project by recognizing the need of training in definite methods of instruction and administration. They adopted the theory that property through a system of taxation should sup-

port the schools. They classified the educational,
financial, and administrative elements in three separate departments of the state system of public instruction.

Nearly a quarter of a century had passed after
the adoption of this educational code before Herbert Hoover enrolled as a pupil in West Branch. By
this time the educational policy of the state had be-
gun to take form. Strong leaders had commenced
to advocate statewide adoption of important principles. Mr. A. S. Kissel, State Superintendent of
Public Instruction, for instance believed that the life
of the nation was determined by the activity of the
school. Accordingly, he favored progressive methods of instruction in courses suited to the need of
that day. It is interesting to note that he advocated
the teaching of Christian morality, especially when
one recalls the fact that when Mr. Hoover as Secretary of Commerce returned to West Branch he
placed in the hand of his former teacher a card
bearing the inscription: "To the real founder of
character, Miss Mollie Brown, from Herbert
Hoover, April 3, 1923." Four decades crowded
with experience could not erase the impression of a
school wherein moral instruction took place.

But we must not overlook the fact that in this
community two compelling influences converged, the
one general, as we have seen, the other specific. The
Quaker families of this rural village were familiar
with and interested in the remarkable work of
Joseph Lancaster of London, England, a member

of their Religious Society who at the very close of
the eighteenth century had started an educational
movement, the influence of which reached to many
parts of the world. The private school which he
conducted for a time in his father's home grew so
rapidly that it became necessary to secure a large
hall on Borough Road near the entrance to which
he posted the following notice:

"All that will may send their children and have
them educated freely; and those that do not wish to
have an education for nothing may pay for it if they
please."

An advertisement carrying such liberal terms
when education was neither free nor public of course
aroused widespread interest and consideration.
Lancaster had developed a plan whereby he taught
the older and advanced pupils, whom he called moni-
tors, how to teach the younger and inexperienced
children. By 1798 he had an enrollment of approximately one thousand children whom he taught at an
annual cost of five shillings each. He had enlisted
the kindly interest and financial support of a few
Quakers who heartily believed in this new and progressive method of instruction. While assuming responsibility for directing the intellectual pursuits of
these children he believed that his duty involved
sharing his life as well as his knowledge with them.
He always considered himself a companion and
friend of his pupils. He often accompanied them in
small groups and on occasions in larger groups, to
places of interest in and about London for instruc-

tion and pleasure. It was natural, therefore, that they should develop a kindly attitude toward, and great reverence for such a companionable teacher.

His school rapidly became the center of public interest. It was visited by some of the most distinguished people of his own and foreign countries. He soon attracted the attention of the King and Queen, who made substantial contributions to his work.

By 1808 his system of education had become so popular that it was necessary to transfer his educational affairs to a group of trustees who, after a short time, founded the "Royal Lancasterian Institution for Promoting the Education of the Children of the Poor." Later, this organization, largely through the efforts of the Quakers under the leadership of William Allen, who served for a time as its honorary secretary, became the British and Foreign School Society. Through the efforts of these founders large sums of money were raised and schools of the Lancasterian type were founded in France, Spain, Italy, Russia, South America, and in the British Colonies, Africa, India, Canada and the West Indies. This organization laid the foundation of elementary education in England by erecting buildings and establishing schools in many of the country towns and cities. In many of these community centers local committees having charge of their management were composed of members of the Society of Friends. This progressive system served to make education a public concern at a time when it was thought best to keep the masses of children in ignorance in order to make their control and government easy.

With this point of view the Friends who saw the good rather than the evil in children could not agree. They believed that the growth of the child could be nurtured through an orderly system of instruction. They considered it the duty of the schools in which they were interested to teach morals and religion but they were open to children of all denominations and while lessons for reading consisted of extracts from the Holy Scriptures, no catechism nor peculiar religious tenets were taught. They believed that public education could have a religious foundation without being sectarian in any sense of the word.

In 1806 this Lancasterian system of education was introduced into the city of New York by the "Free School Society" whose membership consisted largely of members of the Society of Friends. This organization provided education for approximately six hundred thousand children within a period of less than half a century. A close bond of sympathy influenced the acceptance of Lancaster's educational ideals by his fellow Quakers here in America. Soon after the opening of the first school in New York they founded a school in Philadelphia and by 1818 an act of the legislature introduced the system into the state as a whole. In that year the board of controllers began to establish schools for both sexes in the district of Philadelphia. Within a period of ten years more than thirty thousand children had been instructed in these monitorial schools.

During the first quarter of a century after the introduction of the Lancasterian schools into America the system was used with varying degrees of success in many parts of our country. Lancaster himself traveled as far West as Cincinnati, Ohio, lecturing upon the benefits of his educational discoveries. As the people moved into Ohio, Illinois, and Indiana, this progressive educational movement was carried into the West. And as these people came into the state of Iowa, with this educational philosophy as a background they were in a position to favor with determination the public school system which was then being established in that new and rapidly developing territory. Lancaster had proved to the satisfaction of all that public education could be placed within the reach of every child, either rich or poor. Previous to the introduction of the monitorial system into Pennsylvania each child educated at public expense cost the state eleven dollars per annum. The new system reduced this cost to less than four dollars.

Through his methods of administration and instruction Lancaster demonstrated the possibility of teaching children in large groups. Then, too, through his Model Schools, which were first established in 1818, he emphasized the need of trained teachers. This work laid the foundation of our modern teacher-training colleges, which have carried teaching to the level of an honorable profession. The Puritans of New England preserved the range and substance of education, while the Quakers of Pennsylvania made it personal and democratic.

It was an easy step from the Lancasterian System of the first half of the nineteenth century to the state-wide public education system of the last half. It is of more than passing interest to note that the first free school West of the Mississippi River was taught at Tipton, Iowa, within a short distance of West Branch, by John W. Reeder, who came to the state in 1850. As a man past ninety he asked for and was granted the privilege of holding Mr. Hoover's hat when he was inaugurated President of the United States on March 4, 1929.

Because of their historical record in providing free private education, the Quakers were among the first to give hearty approval to free public education. The school then, which Herbert Hoover attended, was part of a state-wide educational system of public instruction which had been influenced by every forward movement in the whole field of American education. It furnished an intellectual, social, and spiritual environment that could have but one result in the life of a child who enjoyed its privileges and opportunities. It took into account the personal needs and aspirations of the individual by considering him rather than the lesson the center of all educational activity. It would be difficult to imagine an educational environment more suitable for the establishment of a social philosophy for the President of the United States than that offered by the community in which he was born. Even the spaciousness of the surrounding territory which was typical and indicative of the breadth of knowledge offered by the teacher and the texts within the walls of the school room compelled independent thought and free action. It had an individualizing effect on the group and a democratizing influence on the individual.

MEMBERSHIP IN THE RELIGIOUS SOCIETY OF FRIENDS

Among the many privileges that Herbert Hoover enjoyed during his childhood days in the quiet and prosperous little community of West Branch, the most significant was that of attending a Quaker meeting for worship wherein his mother, a minister, sometimes spoke. It must be remembered that a minister in the Friends or Quaker church did not hold the same office and carry the same responsibility as persons bearing that title in other denominations. In most churches the minister is one, usually a man who has been trained in theology and church polity in the college or seminary. He is later ordained and given all the rights and privileges ordinarily enjoyed by the clergy. He is employed either by the local congregation or appointed by a Conference or General Assembly. In either case he becomes the spiritual leader of the organization and receives therefrom a yearly stipend or salary. As a result of this arrangement he is expected to prepare and deliver discourses of a spiritual nature on regular and stated occasions. Accordingly he carries a large share of the responsibility of the work of the church which he serves.

Contrasted with this highly organized and centralized institution a meeting for worship of the Society of Friends seems to the average observer somewhat loose and unrelated. In an early day it was customary for the members to gather at an appointed time, enter the building and sit in complete silence until someone felt moved to speak.

Charles Lamb has described a Quaker meeting in the following words: "Reader, would'st thou know what true peace and quiet mean; would'st thou find a refuge from the noises and clamours of the multitude; would'st thou enjoy at once solitude and society; would'st thou possess the depth of thine own spirit in stillness, without being shut out from the consolatory faces of thy species; would'st thou be alone, and yet accompanied; solitary, yet not desolate; singular, yet not without some to keep thee in countenance;—a unit in aggregate; a simple in composite:—come with me into a Quakers' Meeting."

These worshippers were not guided in their religious thinking by a creed that had been written years before by the hand of a state or church official who derived his authority from organizations far removed from the control of the common man. There was no creed and no sacrament except the creed of friendship and the sacrament of mutual helpfulness. Their religious principles were expressed in a series of questions or "queries," usually eight or ten in number, rather than in a set of rigid rules or beliefs. These questions, covering every phase of life, were read in meeting at least once a year. Some of these to which Herbert Hoover listened and to which he gave expression in intellectual and spiritual growth have had a profound influence upon his life:

"Are Friends preserved .in christian love one toward another? Are tale-bearing and detraction discouraged? And when differences arise, are endeavors used speedily to end them?

Do Friends endeavor, by example and precept, to educate their children, and those under their care, in the principles of the Christian religion, and in plainness of speech, deportment, and apparel? Do they guard them against reading pernicious books, and from corrupt conversation? And are they encouraged to read the Holy Scriptures diligently?

Are the necessities of the poor, and the circumstances of those who may appear likely to require aid, inspected and relieved? Are they advised and assisted in such employments as they are capable of; and is due care taken to promote the school-education of their children?

Are Friends careful to live within the bounds of their circumstances, and to avoid involving themselves in business beyond their ability to manage; or in hazardous or speculative trade? Are they just in their dealings, and punctual in complying with their contracts and engagements; and in paying their debts seasonably? And where any give reasonable grounds for fear in these respects, is due care extended to them?"

It early became the conviction of members of the Society of Friends that every man has spiritual contact with the Creator of the Universe and because of such contact he needs neither a creed nor intercessory human agent. Religion was a personal, inward, and vital experience. Any individual attending a meeting for worship either as resident member or visiting Friend had the freedom of the meeting and he could render whatever service seemed fitting and acceptable. He could choose a subject or text as the basis of his message or exhort to honest and honorable living without reference either to so-called sacred or secular authority. There were times during the historical development of the Society that the Bible was not used in the meeting for worship because it was feared that it might hinder liberty of thought and freedom of expression. Freedom of conscience thus became a dominant ideal among Friends. Such a state of affairs soon caused the members to recognize special gifts or talents in young people. When they had spoken so that the meeting was spiritually edified, a committee was appointed to investigate the personal and spiritual qualifications of the one under consideration and report favorably if, in their opinion, the young man or woman should be recognized as a minister. Mr. Hoover would say that they stimulated individual effort and initiative. A person so designated, and there might be several in one congregation, would finally take his place on the Facing Seat. A custom later arose which seemed to specify that the one sitting in a certain place was considered the speaker for that occasion, provided, however, he felt moved to do so. A minister, then, carried the title in recognition of his spiritual gifts rather than in recognition of a professional or educational training in religious technique. Such a minister was not a pastor in the modern meaning of the term. He was not responsible to an organization for his religious utterances except in so far as his message was either considered acceptable to or inappropriate for the audience to whom it was delivered.

It can readily be seen that such a meeting gave the widest possible opportunity for the use and development of individual talents. It not only opened the way for whatever service one might render but it placed responsibility on each person because the gathering could not succeed without a sense of individual obligation.

Mrs. Hoover, the mother of our president, then was a minister by virtue of her spiritual insight, intellectual acumen, and moral responsibility. She was a minister, but not a pastor. Accordingly she was a religious individualist. She enjoyed freedom of thought, speech, and action, restrained only by the effect that such liberty had on the public mind. Under such circumstances either public approval or disapproval acted as a stabilizing or balancing influence. But submission to a traditional belief, custom, or creed could not be demanded by a group of superior officers. There were none. She was the citizen of a country without a king and a member of a church without a bishop.

Just here we must not overlook the fact that while Quaker meetings allowed the utmost freedom, at the same time they required social responsibility. President Hoover's philosophy of American Individualism cannot be properly interpreted apart from an appreciation of this phase of his religious training. Failure to understand his philosophy of friendship leads only to a misinterpretation of his idea of individualism. The activities of his childhood and youth were stimulated and controlled by a friendly idealism. Anyone who believed in the fatherhood of God and the brotherhood of man had a right to membership in the organization. Even a recent document published by a newly organized group of Friends carries a liberal invitation to all who want to be friendly:

"The Association will, therefore, receive in membership anyone who desires to join in worship in spirit, and to seek the truth in the manner which Friends have found most helpful.

"Such a member may retain membership in the particular branch of the Society of Friends to which he may belong, or in any other church if he so desires. He is not asked to believe something or to subscribe to any set doctrine or form, but merely to join in the spiritual fellowship of the Society of Friends."

Many religious groups have considered friendship as merely incidental to the program of the Church. Religious sentiment toward God and an unfriendly attitude toward man have always been associated without seriously disturbing the intellectual balance of the Churchman as he planned and developed his organization—a result undoubtedly of his effort to escape condemnation on the one hand

and to enjoy the fellowship of a pleased Theistic Being on the other. With such a belief the founders of the Society of Friends could not agree. They attempted to bridge the chasm of intellectual error that had always separated religion and morals by erecting a structure called friendship. It was adopted as one of the two central ideals around which a substantial social order could be erected. The writer of the Ten Commandments recognized, if indeed he did not discover, the principle of good will. Unfortunately he stated it in negative terms. The Founder of the Christian religion interpreted the idea and empowered it by crowding it into a compact and positive sentence, "This is my commandment, that ye love one another." The Quakers accepted this as the Commandment referred to in the statement from which they took the name, Society of Friends —"Ye are my friends if ye do the things which I command you." For it was closely followed by a further explanation when he said, "These things I command you, that ye love one another." With this inspiring Commandment, direct and simple, yet elastic and expansive, giving direction to their thought, the Quakers began to correlate this religious ideal with the ordinary law of personal appreciation. They have always believed that a religious law with authority worthy of acceptance should be practical in human affairs. In short if the law, regardless of its origin, is of any value, it must work. This point of view is admirably given in the words of Professor Rufus M. Jones of Haverford College, an authority in social and spiritual philosophy, when he says:

"In the work of bettering the world and of spiritualising humanity, we can no more ignore the structural principles of society than a bridge-builder can ignore the laws of mechanics in his work, but there is no sane and efficient programme which does not include the old-fashioned Quaker faith (not sectarian) in the personal worth of the individual, a faith that a man is more precious than the gold of Ophir, a vision of the potential child of God in the submerged toiler, and, with that faith and that vision, the readiness to identify ourselves as friend with those who need us, the bestowal of personal care and sympathy, the sharing of the self as well as the sharing of money, the cultivation of the spirit of consecration to the tasks and needs of the neighbourhood group in which we live."

In this connection Doctor Henry T. Hodgkin, a leading Quaker educator and religious thinker, has this to say: "The reverent spirit finds its object not only in nature but in our neighbors. Lack of respect for the personality of the other man is a fundamental cause of wars, industrial struggles, race hatreds, educational blunders, family disasters. Nothing is more distinctive of the Quaker view of life than its persistent conviction of the worth of every man, the determination to see and honor 'that of God' in him. This approach to our fellowman was never more necessary than today and perhaps seldom less easy. Prejudices of many kinds are taught and encouraged in family, social group, political party, and nation. Unfortunately the school often reflects and even enforces these false and destructive attitudes. It must be the distinctive task of Quaker educators to send forth persons who have no inner barriers and who approach all men of whatever race, creed, class or nation with an open heart and a deep respect."

The principle of friendship then, has been discovered, interpreted and applied, and so far as a religious society is concerned, it has worked. However, its application has been limited and circumscribed. Whether or not it can be made practical in national and international affairs remains yet to be demonstrated. President Hoover believes that such a policy can be made effective if and when we dare to base both our individual and collective action upon moral law, and make it rather than the yard stick of political opinion, the measuring rod of human progress.

Mr. Hoover, in keeping with the religious convictions of the Society of Friends, has always emphasized the spiritual rather than the material phase of social helpfulness. This is a point that cannot be made clear without an illustration. The New Testament, carrying the story of the life of Christ, naturally relates many of the instances usual, and unusual, around which his social philosophy was built. These stories, some of them called miracles, have been told and retold without number by church leaders in all religious groups and denominations for 1900 years. In many of the stories two points of interest are given. The one is important, significant, central, while the other is more or less unimportant, insignificant and peripheral. When the story is told with the central theme in mind it becomes an incident of spiritual value and social importance. When it is told with the peripheral theme in mind it becomes an incident clothed with materialistic mystery largely without social influence and meaning. John gives us a picture of Jesus and his disciples resting in the mountans. He tells us that the Passover, the Feast of the Jews, is at hand, and there come to the Great Teacher a multitude of people. As he sees them he says to Philip, one of his associates, "Whence are we to buy bread that these may eat?" Philip replies by saying, "Two hundred shillings worth of bread is not sufficient for them that everyone may take a little." Andrew, another of the group, suggests a solution: "There is a lad here," says he, "who hath five barley loaves and two fishes, but what are these among so many." The child had been fishing that day and he had left from his lunch five rolls. He had caught two fish. On his way home he had stopped, as all children would, to exchange greetings with the little group from the mountain side. Would the tired and hungry lad share his food with others? He would. Five thousand men, we are told, sat on the grass, evidently stirred with friendly emotion at the thought of a child giving that which he had to others. Something happened; nobody knows just what. This so-called miracle may never be fully understood nor satisfactorily explained, but of one thing we are certain. There was an unnamed lad there who shared his food with others. For centuries we have emphasized the significance of the so-called material miracle which involved the increase in the volume of bread and fish and have almost completely overlooked the social and spiritual lesson it taught. Few religious thinkers have interpreted the central theme of the story in its application to community affairs, much less world problems. The Quaker believes that the most potent miracles take place in the changing processes of personality and in the control of human conduct rather than in the unusual correlation of material substance such as bread or wine or stones. It is true that the record tells us that "When therefore the people followed the sign which he did they said, 'This is of truth the prophet that cometh into the world.' " But that was an age of signs even though he declared that no signs should be given in order to prove his identity and power. He did not come to confuse the world either by the use of mysterious words or miraculous acts. He had been announced "to preach good tidings to the poor." He had been sent "to proclaim release to the captives and recovering of sight to the blind and to set at liberty them that are bruised." These activities involved a social program based upon the spirit of fraternal understanding and good-will. John, the fore-runner, sent some of his associates to ask concerning the authenticity of his work. "He said unto them, Go and tell John

the things which ye hear and see. The blind receive
their sight and the lame walk, the lepers are cleansed
and the deaf hear and the dead are raised up, and the
poor have good tidings preached to them." Here
then, was a great teacher, thinker, and philosopher,
who was concerned with the needs of people in the
depths of human despair.

He was moved by spiritual motives as well as by
human interest.

He could reply to the lawyer who approached him
with the question, "Teacher, which is the great
commandment in the law" by saying, "Thou shalt
love thy God with all thy heart and with all thy
soul and with all thy mind. This is the great and
first commandment and a second like unto it is this—
Thou shalt love thy neighbor as thyself. On these
two commandments the whole law hangeth and the
prophets."

Supported by such a philosophy that basic social
law known as the Golden Rule has developed into
a spiritually motivated principle that is gradually
becoming world-wide in interest even though it is
not universal in application. Mr. Hoover, who
firmly believes that a president must give moral as
well as political leadership to his people, has called
our attention with striking emphasis to this phase
of our national life. In speaking by radio to the
World Conference of the Young Men's Christian
Association meeting in Cleveland, Ohio, in August,
1931, he said: "No thoughtful person can overlook
the profound truth that the ideals of Christ which

you uphold not only have dominated the course of civilization since His time but are the foundations of our economic and social life today. Because of human weakness, the Golden Rule may have its daily violations, but this great principle, aimed at the common good, penetrates and profoundly modifies all the forces in the modern world in which we live."

SOCIAL SERVICE IN THE SOCIETY OF FRIENDS

The individual who does unto others as he would have others do unto him usually does so because he responds to the compulsion of a kindly and considerate world. Because he is governed by the law of reciprocal rights he puts feeling as well as thought into his program of helpfulness. His acts of service are stimulated by a spiritualized social philosophy. He is not a fanatic because he tempers his zeal with work.

Through acceptance of this ideal, members of the Society of Friends have naturally considered the ultimate spiritual results of all acts having to do with human betterment. The Quaker intuitively knows that there is ever present the temptation to overemphasize the material aspects of social giving because of the selfish interest involved either on the part of the giver or the recipient of the gift. He knows that the spirit of generous consideration expresses itself in spiritual achievement. There was something lofty and inspiring in the words of the Quaker President when on April 12, 1930, he said in his address to the members of the American Red Cross: "It is, indeed, the spiritual in the individual and in the nation which looks out with keen interest on the well-being of others, forgetful of ourselves, beyond our own preoccupation with our own selfish interests, and gives us a sense of belonging to the great company of mankind, sharing in the great plan of the universe and the definite order which pervades it."

That such a philosophy of life furnishes the basis of his own social thinking and altruistic action was indicated in an address which was delivered at the seventy-fifth birthday anniversary celebration of Earlham College, Richmond, Indiana, in 1922. After briefly mentioning the responsibility carried and the work done by members of the Society of Friends during the great plague in London he called attention to the service of the Society during the times of the Civil War, Franco-Prussian War, and the Great World War. He emphasized the fact that many other outstanding organizations engaged in the amelioration of the terrible results of these tragedies under the leadership of Friends. He then observed that "there must be something here more than an accident, that out of a body of perhaps two hundred and fifty or three hundred thousand people of all the world, for the membership of the Friends is not much greater than that, there should have been contributed to humanity during all these centuries that sense of service. . . . It is perhaps unseemly for me or for you to speak of our own, but it is well to remind ourselves for our inspiration and the inspiration of our children that there is here a tradition, there is here the motivation of some great aspiration that follows through generation after generation of our people."

Quoting further from the same address we find something of the scope and significance of the work which was stimulated by the spiritual aspiration of the Society to which he belonged: "During the last war the Friends have served, not alone,—and I am not speaking of myself,—in all of those great measures which have saved from loss of life numbers far in excess of those who have died. If we were to recount the services of the relief of Belgium, the relief of northern France, the relief of Poland, of Austria, of Germany, of Czecho-Slovakia, of Servia, of Finland, of Esthonia, and not even to enumerate Russia we could enumerate over a hundred millions of people who owe their lives today to the intervention of the American people, and in whose representation has been found so large a proportion of the men who have sprung from the Society of Friends, who have had their inspiration from institutions of this character. And the Friends are still in service today. . . . The organization of which I have myself the direction, and in which are associated many Friends, entered upon the scene later than the direct Society of Friends themselves, and in co-operation with the Friends Service Committee we have undertaken the relief that has so far required the service of some sixty steamships, has demanded the entire operative capacity of the railways of Russia for over five months, that has cost the American people upwards of sixty millions of dollars, in order that we might save human life."

Knowledge of these facts prompted Mr. David Hinshaw, author of an excellent article under the title, "Friends of the Truth" in the Century Magazine to say that:

"The most striking recent development of Quakerism in America began with the far-reaching relief, reconstruction and good-will work carried on by Quakers in Europe during the World War and since. The Friends Service Committee during the period of intense and bitter nationalistic feelings worked with all nationalities and creeds and was never under suspicion. The Quakers collected and through nine hundred of their members distributed twenty-five million dollars in war-ravaged Europe and never did they ask in their ministrations whether the recipient was French, German, Russian or Pole nor did they ever consider whether he was Catholic, Jew, Protestant, or Atheist."

Without knowledge of this altruistic tradition of the Society of Friends it would be as hard to understand the present-day philosophy of the statesman, Herbert Hoover, who carried forward the great program of relief during the war without salary or expense account, as it is without sympathetic appreciation to understand the seventeenth century theology of the minister, George Fox, who founded the Society in England in 1652. One cannot review Mr.

Hoover's services on behalf of humanity during and after the war without recognizing the significance of this principle of life. It furnishes the foundation of his political philosophy and motivates his governmental action.

But Friends have not been satisfied to limit service to the sphere of philanthropy alone. They have urged and supported every social reform with which they could conscientiously agree. Edward Grubb, in the following quotation, limits the field of philanthropy and shows the method by which reforms are made permanent.

"Philanthropy, excellent as it is, has obvious limitations. The efforts of individuals, alone or in cooperation with one another, are often found to fail; their field of work is too small, the necessary funds are not forthcoming, and an element of compulsion is often needed which the State alone can supply. The object aimed at can only be adequately secured through changes in the law, and through improved administration of the forces of society. So the Philanthropist becomes the Reformer; the opponents of Slavery, for example, could not be satisfied, like John Woolman, with persuasion; they must have the system made illegal."

A cursory review of the work of the Quakers in this field will show clearly the correctness of this statement.

A little over a decade before the birth of Herbert Hoover, President Abraham Lincoln promised emancipation to four million negroes who were at that time in slavery. This action was taken on September 22, 1862. A year later he declared the proclamation effective and two years later the people of the United States guaranteed freedom to the slaves by making effective the Thirteenth Amendment to the Constitution. It declared that "neither slavery nor involuntary servitude, except as punishment for crime whereof the party shall have been duly convicted, shall exist within the United States, or any place subject to their jurisdiction."

Just a little over a century before President Lincoln's famous proclamation was given and the people of America amended the Constitution, a group of Friends met in Philadelphia and among other items of business discussed the question of slavery. John Greenleaf Whittier, the Quaker poet, says this about the meeting: "The annual assemblage of the Yearly Meeting in 1758 at Philadelphia must ever be regarded as one of the most important religious convocations in the history of the Christian Church." Apparently no member of the Meeting openly defended or even attempted to justify slavery as a satisfactory social or economic system. However, as might be imagined under circumstances which prevailed at that time there were some who were concerned with the limitations or hardships that might be placed upon any members of the Society who held slaves without injury to their Quaker conscience.

As was the custom of the Society of Friends, a committee of four men consisting of John Woolman, John Scarborough, Daniel Stanton, and John Sykes, was named by the Meeting to visit and confer with all members of the Society who owned slaves. From the records of that period it appears that these men performed this service faithfully and well. As they went from community to community they found within the limits of one Quarterly Meeting of the Yearly Meeting (conference) more than eleven hundred slaves. Concerning these visits John Woolman leaves the following record:

"In the beginning of the 12th month I joined in company with my friends, John Sykes and Daniel Stanton, in visiting such as had slaves. Some, whose hearts were rightly exercised about them, appeared to be glad of our visit, but in some places our way was more difficult."

These religious workers always spiritualized their social concerts. They believed that slavery was contrary to the fundamental principles of the Divine order. But at the same time they did not forget the individual slave subject to all of the unfair and unjust demands of the institution of slavery. Motivated by these two ideals, individuals serving under the sanction and with the support of the general body of Friends, carried their message of social justice to the home of the slave holders of America. They not only individualized the negro as the servant of the proprietor, but they individualized their task. It is both intellectually and spiritually illuminating to contrast this type of visitation with that which developed during the Nineteenth Century under the fervent plea of the religious leader as he considered individual salvation the strongest challenge and responsibility of the Church leader. The concern of the Society of Friends was and continued to be social as well as religious. The result of such a message was soon felt in the economic phases of society. Many of the slave holders who were visited by concerned Friends released their slaves and within a period of approximately twenty years the idea of compensating the slaves for services which had been rendered during the period of slavery was well established. The situation in Philadelphia Yearly Meeting serves to illustrate a movement which was carried throughout the length and breadth of American Quakerism during this period.

By 1773 New England Yearly Meeting which had discussed from time to time in its various Meetings the question of slavery, made a record of the following minute:

"It is our sense and judgment that truth not only requires the young of capacity and ability, but likewise the aged and impotent, and also all in a state of infancy and nonage, among Friends, to be discharged and set free from a state of slavery, that we do no more claim property in the human race, as we do in the brutes that perish."

And within a period of ten years no slaves so far as is known were held by members of the Society of Friends in that section of the United States and within another period of five years through the effective efforts of the visiting committees all settlements had been made "between the manumitted slaves and their former masters for their past services."

Within a quarter of a century after the action of Philadelphia Yearly Meeting, New York Yearly Meeting appointed a committee to visit those who held slaves within its limits. In another five years it was considered a "disciplinary offense within the Society to buy, sell, or hold slaves upon any condition." The effectiveness of such means and methods of dealing with problems of such magnitude is seen by the fact that within the next eight years or in 1774 only one slave was to be found within the limits of New York Yearly Meeting. During this same period covering a quarter of a century members of Virginia Yearly Meeting had expressed from time to time their thought and feeling with regard to the problem of slavery. In 1757 they united in condemning the foreign slave trade. A few years later the Yearly Meeting advised its members upon such matters pertaining to slavery, as education, food and clothing. Then in 1768 members of the Yearly Meeting "were strictly prohibited from purchasing any more slaves," and five years later it recommended the release of all males who had reached the age of twenty-one years and of all females who had reached the age of eighteen.

Ninety years before the birth of our Quaker President, or in 1784, the Friends of Virginia directed that all those who refused to liberate their slaves should be disowned by their local Meetings. This action brought an official end to slavery in the

Society of Friends in the United States of America. Their methods of manumitting the slave were in no sense uniform, but in principle they agreed upon three or four definite lines of action. In many instances they made reparations for the services rendered while their servants were in slavery. They carried forward a program of social service which provided education and religious instruction to the slaves for whom they had been or were at the time of release responsible. After the contest had been won within their own ranks they entered heartily into the program of national anti-slavery activities.

Perhaps the outstanding leader of the past century was John Greenleaf Whittier. At the age of twenty-six he was confronted with the decision as to whether he would enter politics or ally himself with a group of men interested in abolishing slavery. On March 22, 1833, he received a letter from William Lloyd Garrison carrying the following challenge:

"My brother, there are upwards of two million of our countrymen who are doomed to the most horrible servitude which ever cursed our race and blackened the page of history. There are one hundred thousand of their offspring kidnapped annually from their birth. . . . This, then, is a time for the philanthropist—any friend of his country—to put forth his energies, in order to let the oppressed go free, and sustain the Republic. The cause is worthy of Gabriel—yea, the God of hosts places Himself at its head. Whittier, enlist! Your talents, zeal, influence—all are needed."

He did enlist and the results of this voluntary action are easily measured when reference is made to facts outlined, some years later, in a letter to one of his friends: "If my health allowed me to write I could make money easily now, as my anti-slavery reputation does not injure me in the least, at the present time. For twenty years I was shut out from the favor of booksellers and magazine editors, but I was enabled by rigid economy to live in spite of them, and to see the end of the infernal institution which proscribed me. Thank God for it."

One of the most interesting and significant incidents in connection with the political life of the United States is found in the campaign conducted on behalf of Abraham Lincoln during the period of his candidacy for the presidency of the United States in 1860. Lincoln's party wrote into its platform a paragraph that unmistakably placed it and him on record in favor of the freedom for the slave. His election therefore demanded the support of people who held new and progressive social theories. It was felt that if he could carry Pennsylvania he would be elected to the high office which he ultimately filled with such distinct honor. In order to carry this state it was thought that it would be necessary to call out the Quaker vote. To this task John Greenleaf Whittier set his mind and his hand and expressed a challenge to his fellow Quakers in the following words:

"Not vainly we waited and counted the hours,
  The buds of our hope have all burst into flowers,
  No room for misgiving—no loop-hole of doubt,—
  We've heard from the Keystone! The Quakers are out.

The plot has exploded—we've found out the trick:
The bribe goes a-begging; the poison won't stick.
When the Wide-awake lanterns are shining about,
The rogues stay at home, and the true men are out!

The good State has broken the cords for her spun;
Her oil-springs and water won't fuse into one;
The Dutchman has seasoned with freedom his kraut,
And slow, late, but certain, the Quakers are out!

Give the flags to the winds! set the hills all aflame!
Make way for the man with the Patriarch's name!
Away with misgiving—away with all doubt,
For Lincoln goes in, when the Quakers are out!"

The Quakers who had practically withdrawn from politics in the state which they had largely controlled during the early period of its development went to the polls in support of Lincoln's ideas.

It is little wonder, then, that President Hoover spoke in this connection with such conviction and appreciation of the great Lincoln at the dedication of his remodeled tomb in Springfield, Illinois.

"Time sifts out the essentials of men's character and deeds, and in Lincoln's character there stands out his patience, his indomitable will, his sense of humanity of a breadth which comes to but few men. Of his deeds those things which remain in the memory of every school child in America are the preservation of the Union, the emancipation of the slaves, the infusion of the new conception of popular government. Those are the transcendent services for which he is enshrined by his countrymen. In these accomplishments Lincoln not alone saved the

Union, emancipated a race, and restored the Government to the people, but made the United States a power so potent in the world as to turn the tide of human affairs."

With an understanding born of similar experience, President Hoover, in his birthday address in 1931, gave recognition to President Lincoln's unselfish efforts to preserve the Union and to liberate the slave:

"Here are the very chairs in which he meditated upon his problems. Over the mantel piece hangs his portrait with his Cabinet, and upon this fireplace is written, 'In this room Abraham Lincoln signed the emancipation proclamation of January 1, 1863, whereby 4,000,000 slaves were given their freedom and slavery forever prohibited in these United States.' It was here that he toiled by day and by night that the Union created by the fathers might be preserved and that slavery might be ended."

In the place of Lincoln sits Hoover today meditating and working upon problems no less significant and no more clearly understood than the issues of his day. He is inspired by the same lofty idealism as he contemplates the magnitude of the task of preserving the government for the people and keeping alive the principle of individual liberty amidst the complexity of our social and political order.

Mr. Hoover is encouraged by more than a general historical knowledge of this phase of social justice. His great, great grandfather had, it seems, because of economic necessity and religious conviction, left North Carolina in 1818 in search of a new home in Ohio. He, like hundreds of other Friends, could no longer compete with the slave labor of his Southern neighbors. More than thirty years before, Friends had liberated their slaves. Gradually but surely they were compelled to leave the South, not because of antipathy to the slave holders but because of their opposition to the institution of Slavery. Many strong and important meetings in the Southern states lost practically their entire membership through removal of their members to southwestern Ohio and southeastern Indiana.

Doctor Louis T. Jones say that "in 1800 the Quakers in South Carolina and Georgia could have been counted by the thousands: in 1809 they were nearly all gone. They 'sold their lands, worth from ten to twenty dollars per acre, for from three to six dollars, and departed, never to return.' "

Finally when some of these people together with the descendants of others heard of the advantages enjoyed by the people of Iowa they loaded their wagons and moved to the northwest. Mr. Hoover's ancestors, as we have already noted, were among these pioneers.

But we must not give the impression that these Friends were evading a social and political issue. Rather they worked with all diligence in their new home of freedom to bring about the liberty of the slave. West Branch became a constructive social center in which all people of the negro race could find assistance in the solution of their problems.

Soon after the Thirteenth Amendment to the Constitution became effective and the institution of slavery was made illegal, members of the Society of Friends turned with renewed interest to another field of friendly service. Our record of their new work begins when Jesse Clark Hoover, in the course of his day's work at his place of business greeted one of his neighbors with the announcement that "another President Grant was born at our house yesterday." This announcement, coming as it did from a Quaker father provokes inquiry concerning his interest in a president with a war record so pronounced as that of General Grant. The statement itself compels anyone interested in historical research to examine the causes of its utterance. He finds there a story of human interest to those concerned with the social problems of our Western civilization.

A little less than seven years before the birth of Herbert Hoover, Iowa Yearly Meeting (conference) of Friends, expressed an unusual concern in the welfare of the American Indian. These original Americans had been pushed by civilization into the open spaces of the territory west of the Missouri River. As the pioneers moved westward either seeking homes in the territory to which the Indians laid claim or on their way to the far West, they aroused the indignation and resentment of these aborigines. From time to time the two groups came into sharp conflict. The national government had taken account of this difficult situation as is evidenced by the fact that a bill was then pending in the House of Representatives which provided for the transfer of the Bureau of Indian Affairs to the Department of War. The Iowa Quakers, sensing the possible outcome of such a transfer, decided to appeal to the President on the Indians' behalf. Accordingly, in September, 1867, a committee which was appointed by the Yearly Meeting to bring in a recommendation covering this subject reported a few days later with the following proposal:

"After a full interchange of views, we are united in recommending to the Representative Meeting, the appointment of a committee to labor for the promotion of peace between the Indians and Whites, as well as the general protection of the aborigines in all their rights, and to encourage their advancement in civilization and Christianity, by memorializing the proper authorities, or otherwise to labor as way may open for the prosecution of the concern. And we would suggest the invitation of all the Representative Meetings of Friends in the United States, with which we correspond, to cooperate with us if way should open with them."

When this report reached the Yearly Meetings held in New England, New York, Philadelphia, Baltimore, Indiana, Ohio, and Western Yearly Meetings they agreed to the appointment of two representatives from each of their respective Meetings, who formed a committee known as "The Associated Executive Committee of Friends on Indian Affairs." This committee, at its meeting in Chicago in December, 1868, under the chairmanship of Doctor James E. Rhoads, memorialized and petitioned

both the Senate and the House of Representatives
and later as a body met with committees of the two
Houses of Congress. Some members of the committee visited the president-elect, Ulysses S. Grant,
and asked that he give them an opportunity to take
charge of the work among some of the Indians of
the West. Grant replied to their request by saying,
"Gentlemen, your advice is good. I accept it. Now
give me the names of some Friends for Indian agents
and I will appoint them. If you can make Quakers
out of the Indians it will take the fight out of them.
Let us have peace."

But members of the committee were not concerned
with a program of proselytism among the Indians.
They were not interested in increasing the number
of members of their religious organization. They
did want to teach the Indians how to live. The territory over which this committee had jurisdiction
and to which they sent agents embraced all of Kan-
sas and Indian Territory. At that time the greater
part of this vast domain was still in a wild and un-
settled state. The roads were mere paths without
the convenience of either bridges or ferries at the
river crossings. The journeys which the agents made
as they left their comfortable homes to work among
the Indians were hazardous in the extreme. But in
spite of the resentment which many of the Red Men
felt toward any who might again invade their territory, they soon developed a warm appreciation of
the Friends who came to work with them. Even
though these agents were surrounded by large num-

bers of Indians unaccustomed to kind treatment by white men they used no force in preserving order and they did not allow employees to carry weapons of defense. The word "Quaker" became a password that would admit a stranger into almost any Indian village at any time. It would be difficult to discover in any of the annals of governmental humanitarian enterprises a more radical administrative change than that inaugurated by the Chief Executive. For some time the government had used as its Indian agents in the great western territory officers of the army who had been assigned to duties under orders of the Indian Office. Under the new plan the armed military officer gave place to the unarmed Quaker business and professional man. In this list of agents we find the name of Lowrie Tatum who later served as Herbert Hoover's guardian and settled the Hoover estate, and the names of two of his uncles— Doctor H. J. Minthorn and Laban J. Miles. It was in the home of the latter at the Osage agency in Indian Territory that he spent his sixth summer where he was introduced by his Indian playmates to manners and methods of the Red Men of America. The work of the Quakers from the very beginning was so successful that President Grant in his message to Congress in 1869, said:

"I have attempted a new policy toward these wards of the nation. The Society of Friends succeeded in living in peace with the Indians in the early settlement of Pennsylvania. They are also known for their opposition to all strife, violence, and war, and are generally known for strict integrity and fair dealing. These considerations induced me to give the management of a few reservations of Indians to them. The results have proven most satisfactory."

The law governing Indian affairs which was enacted in July of the following year provided for the appointment by the President of agents representing other prominent religious denominations both Catholic and Protestant. This personal and non-sectarian interest which he expressed by word and deed aroused the warm admiration of members of the Society of Friends. It is little wonder then, that Jesse Hoover, in wishing for his newborn son the best that America had to offer would predict a presidential career patterned after that of General Grant.

More than half a century has passed since that prophetic incident. History now records the fact that Herbert Hoover, soon after his election to the presidency in 1928, appointed Charles J. Rhoads of Philadelphia as Commissioner of Indian Affairs of the United States of America. It is of more than passing interest to note that he is the son of Doctor James E. Rhoads, who, during President Grant's administration was Chairman of "The Associated Executive Committee of Friends on Indian Affairs." His appointment was of more than historic interest. It was an attempt on the part of the President to personalize and humanize the work of that great department of government in keeping with the ideals which he himself had learned to appreciate as he heard the stories of pioneer achievement among the Indians of the West.

Mr. Hoover, then, with his sense of justice and fair play, acquired even in childhood, has more than a superficial concern in the welfare of people who may be unfairly treated because of race, color, or creed. His social vision penetrates to the very roots of this problem as he individualizes it by looking beyond organizations and institutions to the people themselves.

ECONOMIC INHERITANCE

Perhaps some will now ask concerning the Quaker's attitude toward business. What is the nature of Mr. Hoover's economic inheritance? The social and religious convictions of the Quakers did not become ineffective when they came into conflict with existing economic custom or law. They did not believe in an inevitable separation of social welfare and economic achievement. Very early in the history of the Society leaders gave thought to the problems of trade and industry. Strange as it may seem, in their meetings for worship and for business, questions covering problems of economics were proposed and discussed. That religion could not be separated from business is shown by one of the Queries already quoted. At least two standards of action were set up.

In the first place, members of the Society of Friends have always held that justice and equity should characterize all transactions in the field of business. From the very beginning they believed that a shop keeper or trader should have one price and only one for his merchandise. It will be remembered that at that period in the history of business a merchant might set a price above that which he actually expected to receive and thus have the privilege of determining the superiority of his own sales ability over that of the purchaser. It soon became known that even children could go to the Quaker merchants with the understanding that they would be given the same price for a commodity that would be charged an adult. George Fox, founder of the Society admonished his associates with the following:

"You tradesmen, merchantmen of all sorts whatsoever, set no more upon the things you sell or exchange, than what you will have. Is it not more savoury to ask no more than you will have for your commodity, to keep to yea and nay, in your communications, and here will be an equal balancing of things; so you will come to show a life like Christians. So a child shall trade with you as a man because of the equity, and people shall not be afraid of one cheating the other, or destroying one another."

Such a standard of values and such an ideal of merchandising soon increased the number of patrons and many members of the religious organization grew prosperous and even wealthy. Their emphasis upon simplicity, sincerity, honesty and sobriety sometimes made others feel unacquainted with their business motives and intentions. George Fox leaves this observation of Seventeenth Century practice on record:

"Many Friends that were tradesmen of several sorts lost their customers at first, for the people were shy of them and would not trade with them; so that for a time some Friends could hardly get money enough to buy bread. But afterwards, when people came to have experience of Friends' honesty and faithfulness, and found that their yea was yea, and their nay was nay; that they kept to a word in their dealings, and that they would not cozen and cheat them; but that if they sent a child to their shops for anything, they were as well used as if they had come themselves; the lives and conversation of Friends did preach, and reached to the witness of God in the people. Then things altered so that all the inquiry was, 'Where is there a draper or a shopkeeper or tailor or shoemaker or any other tradesman that is a Quaker? In so much that Friends had more trade than many of their neighbours, and if there was any trading they had a great part of it. Then the envious professors altered their note, and began to cry out, 'If we let these Quakers alone, they will take the trade of the nation out of our hands.' "

In the second place the Quakers, while finding satisfaction in their work wanted the products of their efforts to serve mankind. This ideal has never been easy to attain, but a proper appreciation of the human element in business has helped to accomplish results. Many of the conveniences of modern society are due to the foresight and ingenuity of members of this religious group who were inspired to invent and manufacture articles of usefulness. This desire to serve has made the matter of profit a secondary consideration. The real Quaker has always used money as a means to an end and the end usually involved some phase of human interest. Richard Reynolds, a very wealthy Quaker manufacturer of England over one hundred years ago described in a single sentence the tragedy of misguided financial interest:

"A sordid love of gold, the possession of what gold can purchase, and the reputation of being rich, have so depraved the finer feelings of some men, that they pass through the most delightful grove, filled with the melody of nature, or listen to the murmuring of the brook in the valley, with as little pleasure and with no more of the vernal delight which Milton describes, than they feel in passing through some obscure alley in a town."

The author of these words, during a period of distress in London in 1795, sent one hundred thousand dollars to that city to be distributed among the needy, while he kept four men busy in his own community taking care of his fellow townsmen. It was he to whom George III turned in an effort to have manufactured large orders of cannons for use against the American Colonies and against France under Napoleon. But even at that early date Reynolds and his associate preferred not to sacrifice their peace policy for commercial profit. They would not make money out of war. Life is too sacred for that.

Such examples as this have ever stimulated the high idealism of the group as they have endeavored to help build our social and industrial order. History is replete with incidents of personal financial sacrifice on the part of Friends in their effort to be fair and honest in the realm of political economy. They have always held that a definite relationship exists between the economic order and human welfare. In this principle Mr. Hoover finds support for his present economic policies.

WESTERN CONTACTS

But we must not give Iowa and Iowa Friends all the credit for his philosophic turn of mind, because Oregon and California have made their contribution to his mental and moral development. However, since we are concerned with historical data only as they relate to the main theme of our work we cannot do more than say just a word about the similarity of the two environments. In the very year that all the free land had been taken in Iowa (1875) a number of Quaker families decided to go to Oregon and there establish a Quaker colony. In this they were following a pioneer precedent established by the early English immigrants who came to the Atlantic shores in early colonial times. Even though they traveled by train it took eight days to cover the distance from Omaha to San Jose where they were met by others interested in the Oregon project.

The men of the party soon pushed northward by boat, rail, and stage to Portland from which point they traveled by river boat, horseback, and on foot seeking a location for their far western colony. This they finally found in the beautiful valley of the Chehalem where it empties into the Willamette, twenty-two miles south of Portland, now Newberg.

Soon after their families and friends arrived they followed custom by building a school and meeting house. Ten years later they founded Friends Pacific Academy, the forerunner of Pacific College. To the principalship of this institution they invited Doctor H. J. Minthorn who had served a few years before as head of the Indian School at Forest Grove, Oregon, but who was at the time of his appointment acting in the same capacity in a school in Indian Territory. Of course it was only natural that Doctor Minthorn should arrange to have his nephew, Herbert Hoover, then a boy of eleven, enroll in the new academy, even though it involved a transfer from his farm home in Iowa to the frontier country of the Northwest. The six years spent here and in Salem where he still holds membership in the Society of Friends gave opportunity to continue his experiences and strengthen his philosophy, the foundations of which we have already described. At the age of seventeen he could have come into contact with few men whose vision of life and appreciation of it was more in keeping with that which he had been taught to respect than with Doctor David Starr Jordan, President of Stanford University. But we must not write a biography—Will Irwin has done that.

Because of all these western contacts he could say with convincing sincerity during his campaign for the presidency: "I am from the West, where our people are proud to be the melted product of both the North and the South. Our accent differs from that of the people of Alabama and Vermont, but we have the same hearts, the same kind of homes, the same ideals and aspirations."

Perhaps these facts will give sufficient historical and environmental background to show that Mr. Hoover is the descendant of a long line of ancestors whose ideal of service involved the spirit of kindly consideration toward all mankind. He learned from them that men are not mere abstractions; that they are individual units of a social order. Among them he experienced individualism raised to the high level of mutual interdependence. Association with them gave him a sense of social progress through individual growth and achievement. He developed a patriotically and spiritually motivated faith in this type of structural framework which is at once dynamic and practical. It finds expression in much that he thinks and does for the people whom he serves.

David Hinshaw summarizes the influence of these people upon the life and work of the President, when he says:

"Hoover the Quaker, given to reticence, distinctly modest, quick in sympathy for the oppressed, with great strength and instinctive gentleness and with astounding audacity of the spirit, is full of the manners and methods of this peculiar people. He does not represent Quakerism in its rigid interpretation, but the indelible impressions of childhood have matured into a manhood concerned with the things of the spirit, and the fiber of that spirit makes it pliable but unbreakable."

THE PRESIDENTIAL CHALLENGE

Now when Herbert Hoover, on August 11, 1928, accepted the nomination as the Republican candidate for President of the United States he revealed a personal conviction by declaring, "I come of Quaker Stock." The words were not uttered under a spell of emotional idealism. They were inspired by the prospective responsibility that would fall upon his shoulders in case he became the thirty-first President of our Republic. He well knew that his fellow citizens were interested in his spiritual as well as his social and political inheritance. They had investigated his political background; they had reviewed his social record; they would now inquire into his religious convictions. He evidently was not afraid of what might be found there.

The statement, short and simple, was as challenging as it was startling, as sweeping as it was comprehensive, and as prophetic as it was historical. The sentence in itself, to those who understood its implication, carried a campaign promise that only the most daring could make. Its roots penetrated into the history of the past; its branches lifted beyond the limits of modern materialism. It was a sentence whose "words burned" and whose "thought breathed." In it was to be found the historical background of the philosophy of a man whose vision reached the realm of lofty idealism, while his feet stood solidly on the soil of a free and practical nation.

This reference was not one of political expediency. His habit of mind had been built up through a period of more than half a century of parental influence and community contact. It could not be changed instantly; it did not need to be changed. His was a mind capable of producing a type of moral and political leadership worthy of the support of a people whose major interest is social and spiritual progress. They wanted a president who could recognize the obsolescence of a vast amount of modern political intrigue and religious pretense.

He sensed the unexpressed, though urgent, demand on the part of his fellow citizens that he reveal his spiritual principles of life. He well knew that an intelligent electorate would demand a national leader whose philosophy was supported not only by a platform of practical political principles, by a code of effective social ethics, by a system of progressive educational values, but by a constructive outline of spiritual ideals. Some of these ideals were to be found in the religious principles of the Society of Friends, or Quakers. The challenge then, not only revealed the thoughts of a man, but the tenets of a religious Society as well.

We have tried to examine these principles without political prejudice or denominational bias. We have been concerned with them only as they affect the policies of our people. In no sense have we been interested in their interpretation as they relate to the religious body in which Mr. Hoover holds membership. We have attempted to show the origin of and the reasons for his interest in and his loyalty to certain national ideals.

Soon after Mr. Hoover's election to the presidency of the United States, Doctor Charles Clayton Morrison, Editor of the Christian Century, published an open letter to the President in his journal. It expressed in vivid and concrete terms the attitude of many religious thinkers and it gave expression to an emotional feeling which grew into strong public opinion during the period of publicity immediately preceding the election. He says in part:

"In assuming the responsibilities of your high office as President of the United States you have stirred the hearts of your countrymen with great hopes. . . . There is a widespread feeling that you may surprise us by carrying our national policies to new levels of action. . . . But in a large body of your most discerning fellow countrymen there exists a feeling that in Herbert Hoover the nation has chosen a new kind of President, a man who brings to his high office certain qualities of mind and character which have never before been represented in the presidency, and whose influence upon our national life will therefore write a new kind of chapter in American history. . . . We impute these qualities to you because of your background, because in your earlier years certain fundamental convictions were woven into the texture of your nature, and we dare to believe that these are still among your major loyalties.

"You were brought up a Quaker. In so far as you reflect the Quaker outlook on life and the Quaker virtues you are indeed a new kind of President. You are the first Quaker ever to be President. In you for the first time in any country the Quaker tradition has reached a place of major power. There is something thrilling and challenging about it. And sobering too. Three centuries of this tradition now will seem to find their most conspicuous personification in you. It is your uniqueness that you bring a new religion to the White House, a religion which has a direct bearing not only upon the character of its devotees but upon the policies of government."

Such a statement, coming as it did from the pen of one of our greatest religious leaders, quickly centered the attention of the American people upon the spiritual idealism of our president. Those familiar with the editorial policy of this journal were not surprised at this stimulating expresson of expectation. The editor put into clear and forceful language the thoughts which religious leaders have been expressing ever since the beginning of the modern interpretation of social responsibility in matters touching spiritual expression. Students in this field of research have come to believe that ethical and spiritual principles should not be reserved for the field of education and religion alone, but that they should be applied to problems of government both national and international. This insistent demand on the part of the social thinkers of America then, would naturally be expressed in the editorial columns of this paper. Few American journals have followed the present Administration more closely and scrutinized more definitely and criticised or praised more plainly and honestly than has this journal.

In view of these facts it was of profound interest to the close observer of the President's governmental activities to read in the leading editorial of the *New York Times* under date of July 1, 1931, more than two years after the open letter appeared, and less than two weeks after President Hoover announced his moratorium plan covering war debts and reparations, that:

"Everybody must feel, however, that behind the whole negotiation there are elements and forces which cannot be reduced to money definitions or to estimates in terms of years. Something different, something new and higher, a wholly changed atmosphere, has been let loose by President Hoover upon the world. All men know that somehow the previous status has been radically altered. They cannot tell you exactly how. Not yet have they been able to orient themselves under the new conditions. But they are aware . . . that in the matter of reparations and debts old things have passed away and all things have become new. This is especially true of the attitude and temper in which the nations are now approaching the subject. It is mainly a spiritual change."

CHAPTER II

American Individualism and the Philosophy of Freedom

The Problem of Freedom. The Intrinsic Value of Man. Individual Initiative. Implication of Personal Freedom. Individual Freedom and Social Responsibility.

"What we need today is steady devotion to a better, brighter, broader individualism—an individualism that carries increasing responsibility and service to our fellows. Our need is not for a way out but for a way forward. We found our way out three centuries ago when our forefathers left Europe for these shores, to set up here a commonwealth conceived in liberty and dedicated to the development of individuality.

H. H.

CHAPTER II

American Individualism and the Philosophy of Freedom

THE PROBLEM OF FREEDOM

SOON after assuming the responsibility of governmental leadership, President Hoover was confronted with the problems of a world economically unbalanced, socially disquieted, mentally disturbed, and spiritually confused. He knew well that every period of world history has had its unsolved problems. It is only natural that this should be so, for if such a condition were not possible society would be static. It seemed, however, that he and his associates were called upon to assume burdens larger and more complex than any statesman would have predicted at the time he became President of the United States. He recognized that the solution of these problems would demand of the leaders careful economic analysis, unbiased social investigation, unshackled mental endeavor, and conscientious spiritual introspection. He knew that success would come only through the combined effort of every individual citizen of the nation over which he presided as chief executive. In the main he faced a great human problem. It was, as all human problems are, one of adaptation, adjustment and initiative. It was, in truth, the problem of life itself, always the same in nature but ever different in emphasis. It had to do with the individual on the one hand and the social order on the other. Mr. Hoover states the problem in a general way in the following sentence:

"Amid the scene of vastly growing complexity of our economic life we must preserve the independence of the individual from the deadening restraints of government, yet by the strong arm of government equally protect his individual freedom, assure his fair chance, his equality of opportunity from the encroachments of special privileges and greed or domination by any group or class."

He clearly understands that if the individual were released from the stabilizing restraints of government he would disrupt society while if the government were deprived of the self-reliant initiative of the people it would stifle the individual.

Professor Max Schoen of the Carnegie Institute of Technology, has stated the same challenge in a single sentence: "How society can best function without stifling the individual—and it functions best only when it stifles him least—how the individual can best express his individuality without disrupting society—and he can do so only when he does not disrupt society—constitutes a nice psychological problem for the social philosopher to solve."

We have here a dual problem apparently paradoxical in both form and function. The first part seems to contradict the second and the second the first. And yet if our civilization is to survive, this problem must be understood. It is plainly a question of the relationship between the individual and society.

For nearly a century and a half we have lived under the stabilizing influence of a constitution which guarantees to each citizen life, liberty and the pursuit of happiness. The spirit of this document has been translated through the great system of American education into personal conviction and it has encouraged individual citizens of our country to seek rights, privileges and opportunities enjoyed by few national groups in history. At the same time, the document took into consideration the welfare of our people as a whole. The spirit of social solidarity found expression in the ideal of national security which was thought would guarantee national progress. To discover and maintain this ideal balance in modern civilization is a challenge to the thinker and leader. In short, the opportunity of the individual must not be stifled and the progress of society must not be disrupted.

THE INTRINSIC VALUE OF MAN

Now society cannot guarantee liberty and allow personal freedom unless it, first of all, places a reasonable value upon the individual. Is he or is he not of intrinsic value? Mr. Hoover believes that he is. And many of the best thinkers of today agree with him on this point. He finds in man ultimate reality. At least there is a spark of Divinity

there. His spiritual concept of individualism takes
the form and quality of an historical fact since his
ancestors intuitively held this view generation after
generation. And throughout a busy life which has
brought him into contact with men of all races and
creeds, under varying circumstances and conditions,
he has subjected the theory to constructive mental
analysis which comes through experience and reason.
Speaking from the point of view of the American
pioneer, he says, "Our Individualism is rooted in our
very nature. It is based on conviction born of experience."

With him, therefore, the idea is irrefutable and
almost undebatable.

Let us quote the President's words which form the
basis of his theory of American Individualism and
then submit it to the searching criticism of both the
scientist and the philosopher. In so doing we must
not overlook the fact that to him the inherent personal quality upon which the theory rests is a spiritual reality. He says:

"For centuries, the human race believed that
divine inspiration rested in a few. The result was
blind faith in religious hierarchies, the Divine Right
of Kings. The world has been disillusioned of this
belief that divinity rests in any special group or class
whether it be through a creed, a tyranny of kings,
or of a proletariat. Our individualism insists upon
the divine in each human being. It rests upon the
firm faith that the divine spark can be awakened in
every heart. It was the refusal to compromise these

things that led to the migration of those religious groups who so largely composed our forefathers."

And again he says: "On the philosophic side we can agree at once that intelligence, character, courage, and the divine spark of the human soul are alone the property of individuals. These do not lie in agreements, in organizations, in institutions, in masses, or in groups. They abide alone in the individual mind and heart."

These statements clearly indicate the nature and quality of Mr. Hoover's concept of American Individualism. He is vitally concerned with the social group but he knows that the group is but the sum total of its individual units. Even though he is always genuinely concerned with the progress of democracy he never permits himself to accept the theory that the individual should be used as a means toward that achievement, if it is humanly possible to prevent it, when the use to which he is put is destructive of his own personality.

The two ideas, then, because of a deep conviction, fuse into a coordinated principle of mutual appreciation. As he contemplates the thesis that life is a "social concern and one of authority," and the antithesis that it is an individual concern and one of freedom, he takes the side of neither. His efforts are concentrated upon the problem of synthesizing the two points of view. His contemplations lead him to an acceptance of the theory of fraternalistic individualism. This concept is given point and clarity when once his idea of the divine in man is thoroughly understood. He is concerned with the social group, but it is through the individual that he manifests his interest. It is in this realm that he has made the greatest contribution to modern social thinking.

He believes in a universal personal force, or power that is at once creative, constructive, and cordial. This thought suggests the possibility of the oneness of all life and the interdependence of all people.

And now we ask the scientist for his opinion. Sir Arthur Eddington, an eminent English scholar, agrees with Mr. Hoover when he says, "In him (man) there flickers for a few short years a spark from the Divine Spirit." Professor Julian Huxley, a recognized authority on this subject, says: "The matter of which living things are composed is the same as that in the lifeless earth and the most distant stars; the energy by which they work is part of the same general reservoir which sets the stars shining, drives a motor-car, and moves the planets or the tides. There is, in fact, only one world-stuff, only one flow of energy. And since man and life are part of this world-stuff, the properties of consciousness or something of the same nature as consciousness must be attributes of the world-stuff, too, unless we are to drop any belief in continuity and uniformity in nature. . . . In this universe lives man. He is a curious phenomenon: a piece of the universal world-stuff which as the result of long processes of change and strife has become intensely conscious—conscious of itself, of its relations with the rest of the world-stuff, capable of consciously feeling, reasoning, describing, and planning."

In this connection, Professor Edwin B. Frost, director of Yerkes Observatory, Chicago University, makes the following observation: "The development of a human being is doubtless as complicated as that of a star, but from the atom to the star and from the microbe to the man we can believe that the same divine power holds sway."

But what do the philosophers have to say about all this? One of the most heartening facts of intellectual investigation is a possible correlation between science and religion on this phase of life's activity. Both the scientist and the theologian find the correlating agency in power. Carl Heath, of England, clearly and forcibly proposes the thesis that in the individual this power is personal:

"The whole creation known to us is either a struggle between two forces, the moral and the non-moral, with no guarantee that the moral will ultimately survive, or it is an evolving universe in which the whole creation is mastering the lesson of being and of form, of rightness and of beauty and of truth;—of reality in brief, at and by and through the inspiration of a Power of Life that is friendly, purposive and directive. And indeed Religion carries this further and claims that in so far as we are learning to understand with truer insight the implications of personality, this Power is personal."

Having come to this conclusion, he goes one step farther and suggests in the course of his dissertation that this creative power is inherent or dwells in the original nature of man. In this idea he heartily agrees with Mr. Hoover when he says: "Our individualism insists upon the divine in each human being."

Three conclusions, then, stand out with challenging emphasis: There is a oneness of all life; there is a power of life that is personal; this power dwells within man as a creating, unifying and personalizing force.

If we invite the physicist and the chemist to discuss these suggestions with us, they will at once begin with the theory of the oneness of all life because of the existence of a universal creative force. They will mention energy, out of which comes radiation on the one hand and matter on the other. Under radiation they will discuss items such as electromagnetic waves, light waves, X-rays, cosmic rays, and under matter they will discuss atoms, electrons, protons, hydrogen, helium, and various compounds. We would discover that during the past half century the scientific theory which formerly considered matter ultimate reality had reversed itself. If then, these scientists would show that energy is universal and that it is found in all places at all times under varying conditions in the universe—in wood, stone, iron, water, fire, and in all organic matter—certainly they would convince us that it is found in the human body.

If at this point we would invite the biologist to join the discussion, we would ask the difference between organic and inorganic energy, to which he would reply by saying that there is little or no difference except in method of expression. We would learn from him that it takes a human being approximately twenty years to build a mature physical structure through which biological energy could function. This body, weighing approximately one hundred and fifty pounds, would have the ability to move about as a unit or as an individual. And at some point in the development, he would have the ability to think and feel and will. He would develop an ability which would give him self-control, self-mastery, and self direction. In short, he would have personal power. This something which the scientists call universal energy, becomes personal in personality. It is here that it reaches its highest point of expression.

This power which the physicist calls universal energy the biologist would call life's dynamic equilibrium. The philosopher would call it "inter-related and inter-penetrating continuum." The essayist would call it the mystic bond of life, or perhaps the "organic synthesis of reality." The theologian would call it the divine spark of God. If, then, this energy becomes personal and is found in personality, the individual looks within for ultimate reality—intrinsic value.

Such a correlation of scientific and spiritual ideas makes the theory of the divine spark as held by Herbert Hoover not only believable, but intellectually tenable as well. It would be difficult, therefore, to find a leader in the field of social science whose thoughts are more acceptable to the thinkers in this field of human endeavor. In view of these ideas, what shall we say concerning the implications of this mystical outlook upon life? Just what is the value to human society of the belief that there is something universally potential in the life of every person?

In the first place, if a human being is created and sustained by this universal force he at once becomes intrinsically valuable in and of himself. He becomes an individual because he observes sooner or later that he is a unit of life separate and distinct from all others. This is true because he finds creative processes of life at work within his body. He is growing, achieving. This feeling of personal worth does not, as it might seem to imply, rob him of a sense of social consideration. On the contrary, it leads him to see the same power and processes in others because they too draw on the same reservoir of universal energy. He measures every other person by his own standard of values. He "never uses a man as a means to an end, when the use to which he is put is detrimental to him."

In the second place, this belief centers attention upon the problem of helping every individual to respond to the creative urge or upthrust of his life rather than upon the problem of making him good. The man who finds within himself ultimate reality or something Divine discovers an authority that at least helps to guide moral conduct. Goodness becomes a product of the activities of a growing and expanding personality. Accordingly, the whole program of social advancement is made dynamic and helpful.

And this is exactly what Mr. Hoover believes. "Our social and economic system cannot march toward better days unless it is inspired by things of the spirit. It is here that the higher purposes of individualism must find their sustenance. Men do not live by bread alone. Nor is individualism merely a stimulus to production and the road to liberty; it alone admits the universal divine inspiration of every human soul."

Such a belief, then, results in an attempt to harmonize life with the creative program of the ages while it puts warmth and color into all life processes and gives direction and value to human experience. The individual is related to the cosmic universe on the one hand and to the social and spiritual universe on the other, and yet he has within his personality a power that is personal. Under the stimulus of this scientific and philosophic inspiration society will not stifle the individual. This ideal has always served to prevent the concept of individualism from degenerating into the theory of anarchy. The former is the negation of the latter. An individual by responding to the creative urge within, naturally contributes to the welfare of his associates.

Having reached the conclusion that the individual is intrinsically valuable, and having recognized this value as the basis of all social progress, we are now ready to discuss the three constructive principles of individualism as outlined by President Hoover:

"Humanity has a long road to perfection, but we of America can make sure progress if we will preserve and stimulate the initiative of our people, if we will build up our insistence and safeguards to equality of opportunity, if we will glorify service as a part of our national character."

INDIVIDUAL INITIATIVE

A person of intrinsic worth now faces responsibility as a unit of the social order. Will he disturb this order if we preserve and stimulate his initiative? Will he "so live that the law of his life might well become the law of all mankind?"

In order to understand the first principle of American individualism we must drive our thought back, if we can, to the origin of initiative. Out of what conditions does it arise? Is it selfish or altruistic in nature? Our individual of power and value, as he takes his place in the social group as a conscious unit, faces a world wherein facts must be considered. He is now in an environment of factual relativity. He becomes involved in relationships and at once his individual initiative seeks expression. But can society allow this without running the risk of being disrupted? In order to answer this question we must analyze the sub-soil of initiative.

The real reason why society can allow the growing individual freedom of initiative is because of a high and noble inherent attribute. He has a desire to know right relationships. He seeks truth. Perhaps the scientist has an equal if not better right than any other to express an opinion relative to the truth-seeking attribute of personality, inasmuch as his work is largely concerned with the discovery of truth. Again let us ask Sir Arthur Eddington to help us here.

"If we go right back to the beginning," says he, "the first thing we must recognize in the world is something intent on truth—something to which it matters intensely that belief should be true. We settle that as the first ingredient of the world of experience, before we invite science to take the problem in hand and put in order other facts of experience. If in its survey of the universe science rediscovers the presence of such an ingredient, well and good; if not, the ingredient remains none the less essential, for otherwise the whole quest is stultified.

"What is the truth about ourselves? . . . Let us remember that there is one elementary inescapable answer. We are *that which asks the question*. Responsibility towards truth is an attribute of our nature. It is through our spiritual nature, of which responsibility for truth is a typical manifestation, that we first come into the world of experience; our entry via the physical universe is a re-entry."

This inherent quality gives the individual a right to express initiative because it determines the nature of the liberty which he demands and the methods by which he acquires it. True knowledge always helps a person to understand the nature of his own ability and the limits of his personal rights and social obligation. With Francis Bacon he has a "desire to seek, patience to doubt, fondness to meditate, slowness to assert, readiness to reconsider, carefulness to set in order, and, as being one that hates every kind of imposture."

While this attitude toward life stimulates self-expression, it also compels adaptation and adjustment. It gives birth to orderly processes of thought and action and guides initiative in its promotion of progress. "Our great American experiment," says Mr. Hoover, "has demonstrated that the people will of their own initiative take care of progress if the government can remove abuses and help put the signs on the road, stimulation to all of which is part of the job of president."

But some may question the validity of this conclusion and at once remind us of the number of people who do not have the ability to live on this high plane of intellectual effort. We must respond by calling attention to the high quality of our people. For more than three centuries we have demanded individual liberty. We would hardly have attained it at the price required if we could not now enjoy it. As a matter of fact we have merited the right to have it through our intellectual rather than our physical efforts. Our enterprising forefathers came to America under the inspiration of spiritual and educational advantage. They were not moved primarily by the urge of financial profit. This is attested by the number of schools, colleges, and churches which stand today as a reminder of their cultural interests. In light of these facts we cannot argue that organic sensation, or the desire for food, was of sufficient strength to bring people to America and sustain them in their efforts to build here a new civilization. Nor can we believe that an economic urge often expressed in terms of a vocational ideal with all its driving force had sufficient power to shape our national destiny.

"This unparalleled rise of the American man and woman," says President Hoover, "was not alone the result of riches in land or forests or mines; it sprang from ideas and ideals, which liberated the mind and stimulated the exertion of a people. There were other parts of the world even more easily accessible to new invasion by man, whose natural resources were as great as those of the United States, yet their history over this one hundred and fifty years presents no achievement parallel to the mighty march of the United States. But the deadening poverty of other lands was in the absence of the stirring ideas and ideals which have lightened the path of the whole American people. A score of nations have borrowed our philosophy from us, and they have tempered the course of history in yet a score of others. All have prospered under them."

And again he says:

"If we examine the impulses that carry us forward, none is so potent for progress as the yearning for individual self-expression, the desire for creation of something. Perhaps the greatest human happiness flows from personal achievement. Here lies the great urge of the constructive instinct of mankind.

But it can only thrive in a society where the individual has liberty and stimulation to achievement. Nor does the community progress except through its participation in these multitudes of achievements."

It is true that America is known as the world's melting pot, but even this responsibility would hardly rob us of the ability to pursue and cherish individual liberty based upon mental achievement. A large percentage of our people enjoy the advantages of a liberal education. They have the will to know, to plan, to succeed, and to initiate. Governmental officials often forget this fact. Mr. Hoover does not. He pays his fellow countryman a great compliment by taking this quality of human nature into account as he shapes his policies and executes his work.

IMPLICATIONS OF PERSONAL FREEDOM

A second principle of American individualism involves a consideration of a demand for freedom of opportunity. The urge to know and the urge to act or do are complementary factors in a well-ordered personality. Lacking initiative or the stimulus of a feeling of responsibility for truth, the individual would not desire extensive opportunity. Once a social group becomes interested in stimulating and preserving initiative in its members it must grant opportunity. This assumes the nature of a guarantee of freedom.

But the individual who claims the social right of freedom must of necessity prepare himself for such freedom. There must be some condition under which he earns the right to enjoy freedom. Certainly there must be some effort on his part. A great philosopher once suggested the method of approach when he said, "You shall know the truth and the truth shall make you free." This simple formula makes personal freedom possible even in a complex civilization. It places responsibility upon the person who values freedom or opportunity. He seeks truth through educative processes which have rather definite results. If he accepts the theory that a knowledge of truth guarantees freedom, he outlines a course of mental activity. He asks and answers four questions:

What is the nature of Truth?

What attitude toward self does one assume in order to find truth?

What are some of the characteristics of the individual who seeks truth?

What personal results are obtained?

On first thought, truth might be taken as the most perplexing and mythical word in our vocabulary. However, when rightly understood in the light of all its ramifications, it becomes strikingly simple. Seneca once said that, "the language of truth is simple," and Marcellinus likewise observed that "the language of truth is unadorned and always simple." While it is often considered as a guarded treasure of the educated person, to know truth is the privilege of the average man. A great thinker once said, "My witness is true for I know whence I came and whither I go." Truth to him was a knowledge of right relationships. Doctor Daniel Fox gives point and clarity to this assertion when he says:

"Truth is right relationship. If you get the right relationship to water, it will quench your thirst and cleanse your body. If you get the wrong relationship to water, you will drown. If you get the right relationship to fire, it will warm your body and cook your food. If you get the wrong relationship to fire, you will burn. If you get the right relationship to electricity, it will change your darkness into daylight, turn the wheels of commerce, and send your car spinning down the street; but if you get the wrong relationship to electricity you will be electrocuted. Truth is right relationship. Patriotism is right relationship to one's country. . . . Education is right relationship to knowledge. Ignorance is wrong relationship. Political ignorance means tyranny. Religious ignorance means persecution. Scientific ignorance means intolerance. Business ignorance means disaster. Ignorance always means woe."

If, then, truth is a matter of right relationship, and ignorance is a matter of wrong relationship, individual freedom must depend upon the correlation and coordination of knowledge.

Mr. Hoover observes that: "The weaving of freedom is and always will be a struggle of law against lawlessness, of individual liberty against domination, of unity against sectionalism, of truth and honesty against demagoguery and misleading, of peace against fear and conflict."

History reveals the fact that he who does not

know the value of relationships may become a slave of his environment. He who knows not the causes of disease may become a slave of ill health; he who knows not the causes of poverty may become the slave of industrialism; he who knows not the causes of habit formation may become the slave of neural disturbances; he who knows not the causes of crime may become the slave of law. If then, truth is right relationship and ignorance is wrong relationship, it becomes the duty of the individual to determine what is right and what is wrong. In order to do this he must realize that the appearance of truth may do more harm than truth itself accomplishes.

Honest thinking depends upon the thinker's ability to see and understand the relationships between causes and effects and between controls and responses. Volumes could be written about the losses sustained by the human race because of a lack of understanding of these relationships. The difference between the person who thinks in scientific terms or results and their causes, and the one who does not, is the difference between reason and rationalization. Through rationalization an individual might be able to assign a reason for an act which he has accepted, but that reason may not be the cause in any sense whatever of the act. But since one must have a satisfactory motive for his acts, he must find either a true or a false reason for them. In attempting to persuade society to accept the false basis of thinking, groups of people have developed a most impractical system of ideas.

"We cannot ever afford to rest at ease," says Mr. Hoover, "in the comfortable assumption that right ideas always prevail by some virtue of their own. In the long run they do. But there can be and there have been periods of centuries when the world slumped back toward darkness merely because great masses of men became impregnated with wrong ideas and wrong social philosophies. The declines of civilization have been born of wrong ideas."

It seems altogether probable that if the historian were searching through the records of public executives throughout the generations, he would become convinced after having properly weighed the evidence, that their most serious mistakes have been the result of the shifting of responsibility or the rationalization of an act. The human mind has always had the quality of making an act appear right even though the one performing it knew with a reasonable degree of certainty that it was wrong. It cannot be denied that a person either acting for himself or for the public can substitute an imaginary reason in place of the real reason for the act about to be performed. Perhaps no single item of unfairness stands out in human history more clearly than the popular habit of making religion or the Deity or prominent people responsible for acts which ordinary common sense supported by a process of honest reasoning would declare invalid. Here in the United States we have fallen into the habit of holding the president of our country responsible for acts, events or results for which he is in no way to blame. We persuade ourselves through processes of reasoning that he and he alone is accountable.

People who cannot see the relationship of cause and effect are not able to draw conclusions that square with facts. They can neither take advantage of opportunity nor enjoy freedom. Their outlook upon life is cramped.

But the honest average American citizen does try to think fairly as he faces problems which have to do with his own welfare and that of his neighbor. President Hoover likes to appeal to the common man who knows and appreciates the value of common sense. He knows that such people make possible social and spiritual progress. They overcome difficulties because they understand the significance of each item concerned with an event. They are usually free to act because common sense is a mental disposition which takes into consideration the remote as well as the immediate result before permitting the muscles of the body to begin to function. It is a mental quality closely allied with the inescapable desire to know.

If the individual is ready to accept the challenge of truth, regardless of the direction it might take, if he is willing to allow to this inescapable attitude free expression, he will be interested in accumulating facts, interpreting relationships, and predicting results. This attitude will individualize his personality. But as we shall see in the following paragraphs, it will also socialize him. And by so doing it will make him free.

In answering the second question, "What attitude toward self does one assume in order to find truth?" the individual must think of himself in terms of time relationships. He must regard himself as an historical personality and he must of necessity for his own satisfaction repeatedly answer the question, "Whence came I?" For the man who knows whence he came and whither he goes is of all men most free. Appreciation of right relationships makes him so. He becomes historically-minded.

In the first place, he comes to know that he is vitally related to the cosmic universe in which he lives. The scientist would say that he is a product of the universal creative urge. If he thinks of his body in terms of its material constituents he realizes that in its tissues are chemical substances such as potassium, calcium, sugar and salt. He quickly passes over the consideration of the financial value of these ingredients to the thought of the time which it took to build a body weighing approximately one hundred and fifty pounds. He then appreciates the fact that he can survive only a few minutes without drawing upon the resources of the cosmic world. He must eat and drink and breathe. He must at all times have contact with it, and in fact, be a vital part of it. Out of this line of thinking comes the belief that he, as an historical figure, has inherited the rights and privileges of a material universe. Separately he considers the various creations such as earth and water and air and light good. Collectively he pronounces them very good. He perceives that he has inherited a world that he might use and enjoy and serve. For all this he is grateful.

In the second place, as he thinks of his historical self he does not overlook the fact that he is the product of a social as well as of a cosmic universe. He valuates his personality as he enumerates his ancestors. He finds by mathematical processes that at the time Columbus discovered America in 1492 he had more than four thousand grandparents, and if he allows three generations to the century and surveys a period of history covering one thousand years, he finds so many that he finishes his investigation in amazement. He at once declares that he as an individual is of some historic consequence.

Our third question, "What are some of the characteristics of the individual who seeks truth?" naturally grows out of the answer to the second. The first characteristic is a spirit of gratitude. This is the direct result of a knowledge of personal history.

It appears to be historically correct that people who have appreciated their ancestral heritage have been glad to be identified with the great and noble personages of history. Such an identification in times of monarchial governments gave place to the idea of social and governmental privileges, but the person today who definitely identifies himself with the important people of the past, on learning that he is related to them, develops a willingness to fellowship with common people. His spirit of gracious response leads him to communicate with men of noble and illustrious birth and with men of wide and varied interests, and at the same time with men of poverty and want. Such a person is a democratic individual.

The second characteristic of the one who seeks truth or a knowledge of right relationships is an attitude of tolerance. This is a direct outgrowth of gratitude. Its goal is the establishment or re-establishment of right relationships. The tolerant man is he who is most interested in growth and development of personality on the one hand and restoration on the other. His program of social helpfulness embraces preventive as well as redemptive measures. He wants every other individual to have the same privileges and opportunities which he himself enjoys. He would not even ask that others agree with him in his thinking. He does not complain when his close associates achieve success even though he himself should fail. He supports variety in thought and action. He believes with President Hoover that:

"The Union has become not merely a physical union of States, but rather is a spiritual union in common ideals of our people. Within it is room for every variety of opinion, every possibility of experiment in social progress. Out of such variety comes growth, but only as we preserve and maintain our spiritual solidarity."

When the social group permits variety of action on the part of the individual and the individual fosters unity of action in the group, progress always takes place. Danger arises when the group tries to over-socialize the individual and when the individual attempts to over-individualize the group. At this point unity and variety clash, and if at any point American Individualism fails, it is here. The individual who has developed a tolerant attitude not only grants privileges, but he lends a helping hand. There are men with whom he comes in contact who stand condemned at the bar of justice, censored in the court of public opinion, despised in the circle of moral aristocracy, and persecuted at the hands of disinterested strangers. Toward these the tolerant man assumes an attitude of helpfulness. His tolerance often strikes a hidden cord of manliness in the man who is in wrong relationship with his environment and with people. As the tolerant man travels the main highway of life which often leads through the jungle of temptation wherein some of his fellow associates have lost their sense of direction and their appreciation of moral value, he, in the spirit of kindly consideration, welcomes them again to the main thoroughfare of human progress. Tolerance of this type reacts to the benefit of the one who practices it because it enlarges his social horizon, and by so doing gives him a sense of freedom.

Out of gratitude and tolerance grows the social conscience which is the third characteristic of the truth finder. He who is grateful and tolerant because he knows whence he came develops the ability to think of the advantages and disadvantages of the race which produced him. Even the products of the world are considered in the light of the common needs of all mankind. There is a feeling of togetherness as he shares the fruits of the earth and the needs of society with his fellows. It is this sense of social solidarity that gives to the mature personalities a feeling of interdependence. The individual's social conscience becomes the determining factor in questions of right and wrong. Some writers concerned with ethical and moral reactions hold that conscience is the native and unerring or infallible faculty of moral perception, while others think of it as a kind of "taste faculty" that automatically determines for one the things he should or should not do. Of course, modern psychologists and educators do not agree with this point of view. They hold that conscience is not inborn, but acquired through experience and training. Perhaps we might compromise here and say that our "inescapable responsibility for truth" through growth and training assumes the nature of an educated or sensitized conscience. At any rate, most of us do learn to distinguish the difference between right and wrong as we assign value to action in terms of the motives that impel or the results that ensue.

A close study of Mr. Hoover's ethical and moral principles convinces the observer that this concept of values is the basis of his moral conduct. In times of great stress he does not hesitate once he has determined upon a course which appears to him to be right. He analyzes motives and foresees consequences. Because of this attitude, Mr. Mark L. Requa, a close personal friend, is able to say of the President, "I have seen Mr. Hoover at close quarters, in trying circumstances, and I never have known him to waver for a moment between right and wrong."

He seems to have been able to qualify tradition, custom, conventionality, precept, or even instruction itself by reason. Contemplated action seems to have been submitted to the searching scrutiny of reflective thought which helps to evaluate the motives which impel or the consequences which ensue. Carlyle once wrote, "No grander thing was ever done than when George Fox went forth determined to find truth for himself, and to battle for it against all superstition, bigotry, and intolerances."

He fought against intellectual slavery. He was mentally free. Like George Fox, Herbert Hoover has ever sought to discover through experience and experiment that which makes for effective living. He has always believed in the fitness of things and people as of the present. In finding truth for himself through real and imaginary experience he has always stressed the need of scientific investigation and historical research. Real experience may be concerned with present events, processes, and things. Imaginary experience, while embracing these, may look retrospectively into the immediate or remote past or project into the near or far distant future. When experience is projected into the future in an orderly and successful manner, the process of intellectualization may be said to be in operation. This orderly projection is called reason. Through reason an experience assumes the nature of an opinion, and when an opinion is deeply rooted in the past through reason it becomes an envisioned experience. The envisioned experience in turn gives color and value to life because it has both a drawing and directing power by which it limits and enlarges the circle of freedom.

The public leader, like Mr. Hoover, who seeks truth for himself through experience has found the source of human helpfulness. His sympathies, gained through wide and varied experience, are broad and tolerant; his opinions formed because of careful and painstaking analogies, are sincere and purposeful; his decisions, reached through deliberate study and research, are fearless and final, subject, however to change when new and convincing evidence is available or produced. He neither conforms nor rebels. He shares the common feeling and thought of his age. He helps to give poise and direction to the group with whom he is associated or to the nation in which he enjoys citizenship. He is a socially minded individual. He has a social conscience to which he refers all matters of group concern. He cannot enjoy freedom derived through a search for truth and be a selfish individualist.

Gratitude, tolerance, and social mindedness, then, are some of the characteristics of the man who takes time and gives thought to the problem of truth. Equipped with these qualities developed through a knowledge of his historical background, the individual is able to project his personality into the future. He properly evaluates freedom. He looks forward with a vision colored by all the intellectual responses and emotions that have grown out of a retrospective survey.

We come now to the point where we are able to answer our fourth question, "What personal results are obtained through familiarity with and knowledge of relationships?" The answer to this is found in the suggestion that the socially minded individual is free to organize life's activities. He is free to initiate, think out, and carry through plans. This we believe is the sacred right of every American citizen. It is the crux or pivotal point of American Individualism.

Society, in order to make progress, must accept definite aims, some of which are immediate and others remote. These aims must of course become the aims of the individual. For instance, the constitution of the United States is of greatest value mainly as it is interpreted in the life of each citizen of the Republic. As a national aim it is expressed in a document but as an individual ideal it must be expressed in a conviction. As a written document its meaning must be communicated to the citizens of the nation by means of intellectual processes, but as an ideal or an aim for each citizen, its spirit must be communicated through emotional responses as well as by means of intellectual contacts. The individual who has accepted well established aims can form his plans so as to reach the imagined goal in the shortest possible time, with the most economical expenditure of energy, and in the most effective manner. An aim prevents deviation from a chosen course of action, or it acts as a stimulus in denying place to irrelevant activities that might tend to defeat the success of any mental undertaking.

A characteristic life aim must be definite and at the same time flexible. It will help the individual to arrange what he has acquired in an order that will be intelligible, and because of this orderly arrangement will facilitate the choice of alternatives in times when decisions are necessary. It will also stimulate achievement.

We must at once admit that an aim or purpose would be of little value unless there were opportunity to use it. This opportunity for individual planning, then, is the central ideal of American Individualism. It guarantees to every citizen the right to aspire to grow and to achieve. But it obligates the one having such rights to assume an attitude of helpfulness toward others.

INDIVIDUAL FREEDOM AND SOCIAL RESPONSIBILITY

The third principle of American individualism involves a consideration of the social nature of our people. Mr. Hoover believes that we must "glorify service as a part of our national character." This being true, we need to correlate, if we can, the theory of individualistic freedom and that of social responsibility.

Here in America we have been at work for more than three hundred years building a new civilization. Moral standards peculiar to our needs have evolved in the process. The ideals which stimulated our fathers have grown in keeping with the ever increasing complexity of our social order.

We have conducted a national experiment in individual expression that has permitted the idea of individual liberty to grow in keeping with our ever increasing compactness. We set out to conquer the frontier. This we have done. Because of this conquering idealism we have gained the right to have individual opportunity. We take it for granted. It is now a part of the funded capital of American civilization. We did not inherit the ideal; we constructed it. We forged it on the anvil of human experience.

But now that the pioneering is done we must give attention to the serious work of building compact communities. The greatest immediate need is that of a community philosophy which will allow equitable social, commercial and industrial development. Aggressive individuals can no longer move into the open spaces of our country in order to find opportunity free from the restraint of neighborly obligation. We must now develop our individualism in the midst of a crowded and complex social situation. But it must not be a cold and calculating individualism. It must be made warm and vital through our willingness to render service.

In this connection Mr. Hoover has this to say:

"No doubt, individualism run riot, with no tempering principle, would provide a long category of inequalities, of tyrannies, dominations, and injustices. America, however, has tempered the whole conception of individualism by the injection of a definite principle, and from this principle it follows that attempts at domination, whether in government or in the processes of industry and commerce, are under an insistent curb. If we would have the values of individualism, their stimulation to initiative, to the development of hand and intellect, to the high development of thought and spirituality, they must be tempered with that firm and fixed ideal of American individualism—*an equality of opportunity*. If we would have these values we must soften its hardness and stimulate progress through that sense of service that lies in our people."

Sympathetic responsibility postulates the segregation of people into units. That is to say, in order to be social-minded we must at the same time be unit-minded. A good synthesizer is usually a good analyzer. A social-minded person individualizes the mass. One of the difficulties often encountered in a civilized social order is the lack of ability to take a generous attitude toward people of other races or nationalities when they are considered en masse. To the group as a whole we ascribe the quality or qualities we have found in a limited number of its members particularly if they appear objectionable. And if there is already a prejudice toward the group that prejudice stimulates the formation of an opinion based upon the low level of the individual's acts rather than upon the high level of his general tendencies and aspirations. By such methods we form concepts of other people. We become acquainted with only a few persons and then through generalization we attribute the characteristics of the few to the many and form a favorable or unfavorable attitude toward the group. By using general terms in describing people who belong to a certain profession we sometimes dehumanize the entire group. The use of such terms as capital and labor when reference is made to people, is likely to carry impersonal suggestions neither complimentary nor helpful.

If we could individualize the person who finds himself at the mercy of public opinion many times our spirit of ungracious criticism would take the form of intelligent tolerance. Whenever the individual is considered as a symbol he becomes subject to the temporary emotions or feelings of his fellow associates rather than to their generous social reasoning. The supreme test of a social personality is one's ability to see his persecuted or praised fellow citizen as an individual. One of the redeeming features of our age of advanced thought and liberal action is discovered in this connection. We are thinking more and more about people with their likes and dislikes, wealth and poverty, achievements and failures, as individuals, rather than as impersonal units under the control and direction of mythical organizations. When nations develop leaders through whom they can express this idealism, a development of the spirit of social solidarity and understanding will be possible.

Our American social philosophy consists of a set of rules, a code of ethics, or a blue-print of social life. Its essence is mutual helpfulness. A man without a social philosophy can no more be an individualist than a "man without a country" can be an internationalist. For this reason Mr. Hoover's social philosophy makes him a fraternalistic individualist.

"Individualism cannot be maintained," says he, "as the foundation of a society if it looks only legalistic justice based upon contracts, property, and political equality. Such legalistic safeguards are themselves not enough. In our individualism we have long since abandoned the laissez-faire of the 18th Century—the notion it is 'every man for himself and the devil take the hindmost.' We abandoned that when we adopted the ideal of equality of opportunity—the fair chance of Abraham Lincoln. We have confirmed its abandonment in terms of legislation, of social and economic justice—in part because we have learned that it is the hindmost who throws the bricks at our social edifice, in part because we have learned that the foremost are not always the best nor the hindmost the worst—and in part because we have learned that social injustice is the destruction of justice itself. We have learned that the impulse to production can only be maintained at a high pitch if there is a fair division of the product. We have also learned that fair division can only be obtained by certain restrictions on the strong and dominant. We have indeed gone even further in the 20th Century with the embracement of the necessity of a greater and broader sense of service and responsibility to others as a part of individualism."

He believes that a person must develop a sound basis of individual personality as he mingles with others before he can claim the power of social insight and appreciation. He recognizes the simple truth that a man cannot properly evaluate the life of another until he has taken stock of his own personal qualities. If the individual considers himself intrinsically valuable he will without doubt consider others of equal importance. If, on the other hand, he considers himself of little or no consequence, he will without question measure others by the same social yardstick. The individual then becomes the unit of the social order and the social order in turn is formed and shaped by the units which give it life. Society then becomes great only as it gives opportunity for the development of greatness in the individual. Mr. Hoover states this fact in clear and concise terms. "Progress of the nation is the sum of progress in its individuals."

Such a state of affairs demands that every American citizen shall develop for himself a philosophy that brings security to himself and to every other person while at the same time each enjoys freedom of initiative, expression, and achievement. Such security is found in moral law. It is the result of service which must be stimulated by the group and appreciated by the individual.

But in order to understand moral law, the so-called structural principle of society must be outlined and understood. Observers of modern social trends readily recognize the stabilizing effect of mutual helpfulness in our complex social order. It is the framework of our civilization. It cannot be appreciated nor applied to the problem of building a human society until it is analyzed in terms of its component parts, the first of which is sympathy.

A review of the historic reactions and responses of humanity reveals two types of sympathy, organic and reflective. These have been coexistent, but not coextensive nor co-equal. From the psychological point of view organic sympathy is a feeling that exists among members of the same species. It is a natural and spontaneous urge or impulse which holds together members of the same group. It exists among animals as well as among men. It is the result of suffering the same disadvantages on the one hand or enjoying the same advantages on the other. Accordingly, it is largely the product of environment rather than of thought or reason. It moves the group toward responses beneficial to their existence, preservation, and growth.

The autobiography of a criminal who started his so-called career at the age of eight and who has spent ninety per cent of his life within prison walls, shows that he clearly recognizes this important reaction even though he does not analyze it from a psychological point of view. In discussing prison riots he says:

"I have been through three prison riots and I think I know something of how they start. They talk of plots among prisoners, but I never knew of one and those I have taken part in seem to have arisen spontaneously. In each case there has been a growing dissatisfaction among the inmates over food which everybody feels at the same time. They do not have to communicate it to each other. Then somebody starts something and nobody needs a cue to join in. Things simply come to a climax for everybody. The last prison riot I was in came to a head when they served dried raisins full of grit for supper. Everybody seemed to start throwing dishes all at once."

Animals having the same bodily structure, the same needs and capacity for the same reactions, may suffer the same disadvantages or enjoy essentially the same advantages. Old men sympathize with old men, young men with young men, rich men with rich men, poor men with poor men, black men with black men, white men with white men, Americans with Americans, Asiatics with Asiatics, and Orientals with Orientals. The essential nature, then, of organic sympathy is special and limited, confined to a class or group. It is inherent in the situation and its essential quality is emotional in nature.

This type of sympathy has held together the tribe, the clan, and the village, each of which consists of a group of people having a name and an organization usually directed by an hereditary chieftain. The first two are bound by ties of kinship, while the latter is limited by territorial surroundings. Throughout the ages the two objectives have been food-getting and security. The clan is limited and exclusive in nature and organization and its philosophy is narrow and circumscribed. It cannot be otherwise for it thinks only in terms of its own welfare. That is the purpose of its compactness. Within this limited group organic sympathy seems to function fairly well. In such an organization the good of the group naturally takes precedent over the individual. But at this point we need to inquire into the attempt of the larger society to organize itself on this rather selfish basis. Can it be done? We think not. The clan has given place to the tribe, the tribe to the village, the village to the community, the community to the county, the county to the state, the state to the nation, and now the nation must permit world organization and fellowship.

This cannot be accomplished through organic sympathy alone; it must call to its aid that higher and more significant mental, social, and spiritual response called reflective sympathy. This type of response is emotional as well as intellectual. It is a combination of thought and feeling. To rob sympathy of its emotional quality would be to destroy the warmth of its motive power, while to rob it of its rational quality would be to destroy the sanity of its directive force. Reflective sympathy is the result of education, of training, of thinking, which considers facts, theories, and principles objectively as well as subjectively. Its aim is consolidation, its function is socialization and its ideal is mutual helpfulness. It is attained only by individual effort. Through reflective thought one is able to sympathize with people in the depths of human despair and distress, with people of wide and varied interests and with people in the height of human achievement.

Civilization has evolved to the point where it appears comparatively easy for the successful person to sympathize with the one in the depths of despair. Social service agencies are devoting millions of dollars and vast amounts of energy to the relief of suffering in our great metropolitan areas. Organizations such as the American Red Cross are giving relief wherever the need arises, whether in this country or abroad.

Hospitals have been built and maintained for the purpose of relieving physical and mental sickness. Everywhere farms have been purchased and equipped to care for those without sufficient financial resources. Sympathy of this type resulting in activities of this character has developed in the world an altruistic spirit that, generally speaking, has raised people to a high level of mutual understanding. However, it has always faced and many times experienced an undemocratic authority existing under a system of paternalistic government. A proper coordination between a philanthropic ideal and governmental action is difficult to attain. This is one of the reasons why philanthropy should be conducted under the stimulus of private rather than governmental direction.

Looking at the same problem from the standpoint of the recipient of philanthropy, the individual has learned to sympathize with others in the height of human achievement. Obedience to authority has been accepted along with the benefits derived from people in places of control. By virtue of this attitude on the part of the masses, leaders have gained positions of social and economic independence. In some parts of the world the theory of the divine right of kings was accepted because the people had sufficient sympathy with those in authority to give them unlimited power. It is not difficult to follow a great leader, especially if there is some guarantee of support or protection in the program which he outlines. Our sympathy is easily aroused. Under such circumstances it assumes an attitude of admiration and even worship. Men and women everywhere have sympathized with others in this high realm of human endeavor and achievement only to discover at times that these leaders were resorting to the practice of self aggrandizement at the expense of popular welfare. Democratic government has sought to correct this possible evil by limiting the term of service of public officials and by subjecting their decisions to the public will through the ballot.

We recognize the value of these two mental and emotional attitudes but the time has arrived when we need to think of sympathy on a horizontal rather than a perpendicular plane. The question naturally arises as to whether individuals in modern society will now be able to learn to sympathize with others whose interests, ideals, and aspirations are either similar to or at variance with their own. Our system of education on the one hand and government on the other support the idea that we are to look out with rather than either up to or down upon people. Such a sympathetic outlook lays the foundation for the development of good fellowship out of which finally comes good will. And when good will expresses itself in cooperative action it usually takes on the nature and quality of aggressive good will— a will to assist or serve. American Individualism as we understand it, has grown out of this emotional and intellectual outlook on the part of the people of America.

In studying this phase of life we learn that wherever reflective sympathy is in operation there is always a tendency to express it in action. To this extent it is dynamic and constructive. A people cannot have such an outlook without centering attention upon a definite program. This action crystallizes into service because a person cannot sympathize with another without attempting to serve. Reflective sympathy inevitably paves the way for service. If a person does not want to serve he must not sympathize. The one follows the other as night the day because it is through service that the emotion of sympathy finds satisfactory expression. President Hoover appreciates the significance of the need of service among our people to the extent that he believes that stimulation to service is one of the duties of government as it relates to the success of the individual. He has reminded the American people of the necessity of voluntary action in the field of mutual helpfulness. He believes that organizations and institutions should be encouraged to meet the needs of the individual in the realm of service. In this connection he says:

"When we traverse the glorious deeds of our fathers, we today never enumerate those acts that were not rooted in the soil of service. Those whom we revere are those who triumphed in service, for from them comes the uplift of the human mind."

It is in this field that Mr. Hoover's philosophy of individualism reaches a level of life upon which humanitarians like to dwell. His idea of service has been one of the most steadying influences upon American life during this period of social and economic unrest.

With the following words he challenges the leadership of America to a new and important program of service. "We need disinterested public service, moral and spiritual leadership in America rather than the notion of a country madly devoted to the invention of machines, to the production of goods and the acquisition of material wealth."

By way of summary, then, let us say that; An American individualist is a person who, having learned of the intrinsic value of man and having found within himself an inescapable desire to know right relationships, has developed a spirit of gratitude, an attitude of tolerance, and a social mind, to all of which he gives expression in an inclusive program of friendly service.

Such a person will not disrupt society because his plans will be in keeping with the best interests of the group and if society consists of this kind of people it will not stifle the individual because it will desire his freedom. American individualism in its highest form gives to man the position and privilege to which his intrinsic worth entitles him and asks only that he "so live that the law of his life might well become the law of all mankind."

In his 1930 Gettysburg address, part of which might well be framed and hung by the side of that delivered by Lincoln in celebration of the same event some years before, President Hoover crowds into a single paragraph a message that should stir the deepest emotions and arouse the highest aspirations of all citizens of our republic. It summarizes all that has been said in this chapter about American Individualism and the philosophy of freedom:

"The things of the spirit alone persist. It is in that field that the nation makes its lasting progress. To cherish religious faith and the tolerance of all faith; to reflect into every aspect of public life the spirit of charity, the practice of forbearance, and the restraint of passion while reason seeks the way; to lay aside blind prejudice and follow knowledge together; to pursue diligently the common welfare and find within its boundaries our private benefit; to enlarge the borders of opportunity for all and find our own within them; to enhance the greatness of the nation and thereby find for ourselves an individual distinction; to face with courage and confident expectation the task set before us, these are the paths of true glory for this nation. They will lead us to a life more abounding, richer in satisfactions, more enduring in its achievements, more precious in its bequests to our children—a life not merely of conflict, but filled with the joy of creative action."

CHAPTER III

American Individualism and the Functions of Government

Individualism—a Way of Life. Ordered Liberty. Democratic Justice. Intellectual Welfare. Equality of Opportunity. Stimulation to Service.

"*Successful democracy rests wholly upon the moral and spiritual quality of its people. Our growth in spiritual achievements must keep pace with our growth in physical accomplishments. Material prosperity and moral progress must march together if we would make the United States that commonwealth so grandly conceived by its founders. Our government, to match the expectations of our people, must have constant regard for those human values that give dignity and nobility to life. Generosity of impulse, cultivation of mind, willingness to sacrifice, spaciousness of spirit—these are the qualities whereby America, growing bigger and richer and more powerful, may become America great and noble. A people or government to which these values are not real, because they are not tangible, is in peril. Size, wealth, and power alone cannot fulfill the promise of America's opportunity.*"

H. H.

CHAPTER III

American Individualism and the Functions of Government

INDIVIDUALISM—A WAY OF LIFE

AMERICAN Individualism is not a form of government, it is a way of life. It involves every physical and mental activity of a people who are concerned with the development of a liberal political philosophy. Individualism is not a tool of government. It is a spiritual principle upon which the government rests. Out of the compelling ideas of American Individualism democracy came forth as a governmental idea. "Democracy," says President Hoover, "is merely the mechanism which individuals invented as a device that would carry on the necessary political work of its social organization. Democracy arises out of individualism and prospers through it alone."

While granting rights and guaranteeing protection to the individual, democracy does not overlook the social nature of people. It attempts as no other form of government to allow the individual to succeed so long as he does not disrupt society, and permits society to make progress so long as it does not stifle the individual.

A government which assumes the responsibility of

fostering among its people this specific way of life must of necessity be liberal in both form and function because it must adapt itself to the changing conditions of a people of ever changing needs. Adjustments must be made sometimes without the guide of precedents and the authority of universally accepted rules. It considers only living issues. It is moved by personal need on the one hand or human aspiration on the other. The typically American way of life characterized by simplicity, frugality, honesty, sobriety, justice, and liberty naturally demands a government under the control and direction of the people. This concept of American Individualism, a way of life, and of democracy, a form of government, at once outlines the privileges and duties of the individual and defines the responsibilities of the government.

If the breakdown of American Democracy ever occurs it will be because a majority of our people come to believe that the government can do for them what they cannot do for themselves. To overestimate the ability of the individual and underestimate the strength of the government leads to the development of selfish, egoistic, or anarchistic trends, while to overestimate the strength of the government and underestimate the ability of the individual paves the way for the establishment of an autocratic, bureaucratic, or imperialistic control. To properly evaluate both the individual and the government is not an easy task even for the student of political economy, but to let certain principles of government evolve out of individual and group experience and then recognize them as reasonable rules of social conduct should not be too difficult even for the citizen of average public interest. From time to time President Hoover has tried to throw some of these principles into bold outline in order that we might become familiar with governmental policies which are in tune with our past and present manner of life. He holds that successful democracy rests wholly upon the shoulders of individual citizens who are capable and willing to bear both private and public responsibility.

In order to get a clear perspective of this responsibility, let us inquire into his governmental philosophy and see, if we can, whether or not it squares with modern ideals of social practice. On this subject he has a definite proposal to make. He classifies the functions of government:

"We have grown to understand that all we can hope to assure to the individual through government is liberty, justice, intellectual welfare, equality of opportunity and stimulation to service."

These five political requirements are worthy of review and re-valuation. We cannot overemphasize the necessity of a continuous effort in this field of American statesmanship.

Two observations should be made before we discuss these governmental duties.

In the first place, we must remember that this study is concerned with the government and the individual. Mr. Hoover has clearly recognized other governmental responsibilities. The following statement, for instance, helps to make this clear:

"There are three potential fields in which the principles and impulses of our American system require that government take constructive action. They comprise those activities which no local community can itself assume and which the individual initiative and enterprise of our people cannot wholly compass. They comprise leadership of the government to solve many difficult problems. The first of these fields includes the great undertakings in public works such as inland waterway, flood control, reclamation, highways, and public buildings.

"The second of these is the necessary interest and activity of the Federal Government in fostering education, public health, scientific research, public parks, conservation of national resources, agriculture, industry, and foreign commerce.

"The third great field lies in broadening the assistance of the government to the growing efforts of our people to cooperation among themselves to useful social and economic ends."

In the second place, we need to recall a statement in which he shows the limitation of our system of social control. He knows as does every other executive that, "One of the difficulties in social thought is to find the balance of perspective." While Secretary of Commerce he made the following observation:

"It is easy to arraign any existing institution. Men can rightly be critical because things have happened that never ought to happen. That our social system contains faults no one disputes. One can recite the faulty results of our system at great length; the spirit of lawlessness; the uncertainty of employment in some calling; the deadening effect of certain repetitive processes of manufacture; the 12-hour day in a few industries; unequal voice in bargaining for wage in some employment; arrogant domination by some employees and some labor leaders; child labor in some states; inadequate instruction in some areas; unfair competition in some industries; some fortunes excessive far beyond the needs of stimulation to initiative; survivals of religious intolerance; political debauchery of some cities; weaknesses in our governmental structure. Most of these occur locally in certain regions and certain industries and must cause every thinking person to regret and to endeavor. But they are becoming steadily more local. That they are recognized and condemned is a long way on the road to progress."

ORDERED LIBERTY

We have already discussed the nature of liberty when considered from the general point of view of the individual. We must now inquire into its significance as the first function of government. For more than three centuries the American people have demanded individual freedom. As already shown, through our intellectual efforts we have merited the right to have it, even though it has gradually changed in nature and extent.

A century ago the person who valued freedom above all other personal privileges could seek the open spaces of the West and find a condition that liberated him from the legal jurisdiction of the government, released him from the intellectual influence of the school and freed him from the religious inspiration of the Church. He was socially and politically free. He could initiate plans and carry them to completion without interference on the part of others. But when these institutions were organized, control was set up and this type of freedom ceased. Of course the transition from the former to the latter social condition was gradual and almost imperceptible. It was a transition from an absolute state of freedom to a state of ordered freedom, the kind of freedom which Mr. Hoover often mentions in his messages to the people.

He understands that a society, wherein ordered freedom is accepted as a mode of life, requires of every normal individual well defined aims which involve vision, incentive and the use of sound judgment which postulate both adaptation and self-direction. A person thus equipped may justly demand the right to freedom of expression and freedom of action because these will always be subservient to the ideal of balanced processes in both thought and action. The individual becomes an individual because of this ability to limit and at the same time control his activity according to the principles of mental, physical, and social growth. Absolute freedom has always lacked restraint, both social and individual, but it has also lacked privilege, the privilege of mutual cooperation and helpfulness. Ordered freedom allows an even balance of restraint and privilege. It involves liberty which at once grants opportunity and demands an assumption of responsibility out of which grows self-restraint and self-reliance. Such a philosophy growing out of human experience puts warmth and spirit into the idea of individualism. This freedom simply means that every person shall have the right to respond to his environment as the cosmic and spiritual laws of life require or permit.

When an individual begins to make plans because of the liberty which he enjoys he assumes responsibility, for there are few, if any, plans which do not involve limitation of time, space, and effort. These limitations at once influence the acceptance of duty which demands restraint—not from without but from within—self-restraint. This does not mean that all restraint capable of functioning successfully in a democratic society comes from within, but it does mean that ordered freedom largely depends upon the ability of individuals to restrain themselves. Self-restraint, developed and controlled through a course of action, which demands that the individual bears a reasonable responsibility, builds the framework of that necessary quality in the successful individual known as self-reliance. The two terms, self-restraint and self-reliance, become complementary factors in personality. Neither society nor the individual can prosper if either of these qualities is lacking, because, says Mr. Hoover, "No civilization could be built or endure solely upon the groundwork of unrestrained and unintelligent self-interest."

One is the negative and the other the positive phase of human initiative. Restraint motivated by a sense of duty in carrying forward some plan or series of plans, becomes dynamic, purposeful, and constructive. Restraint from within is usually flexible and active while restraint from without is often rigid and static. A democratic social order requires both types of control but its success in the realm of government can be measured in terms of the number of people who accept the idea of individual initiative under the guidance of self-restraint and self-reliance as of fundamental importance in social progress.

Only a small percentage of the people at any given period should require control through governmental agencies. Under the stimulus of a system of universal education such qualities as self-control, self-mastery, and self-direction should become almost universally applicable in human affairs. However, democratic legislators and executives must consider maladjusted individuals made so because of physical and mental defects or environmental carelessness. Such people not only need control but assistance. And just here we discover a democratic principle of the greatest value. Whenever people voluntarily request assistance from the state or because of faulty adjustment require it, the government must have a proportionate right of control. At any rate such has been the history of governmental assistance. As a matter of fact, when the individual demands too much assistance or control, he loses the right to be an individual. He becomes a ward.

In this connection modern American civilization faces one of its most serious problems. We are not making sufficient distinction between the problems which should claim the attention of, and be solved by the individual or small group of individuals and those which are governmental in nature. We are resolving too many private and local problems into political issues. Already our nation has gone too far in this direction and unless attention is given to the political suggestions of our statesmen and a start made to correct our errors we shall have developed within a very few years a system of collectivism that will at once place our governmental representatives in a position where they, because of the nature and scope of their work and office will assume more and more control of our private affairs. If we ask governmental assistance in private matters we must expect it in control of private conduct.

In the final analysis the American people want neither slavery in industry nor paternalism in government. Unnecessary collective interference with individual opportunity, or private initiative, either by corporate business or government, is contrary to the foundation ideals of our country. The government must not destroy individual liberty in this way.

Now if we are to maintain our American ideal of freedom of expression and personal growth, we must give increasing attention to the functions of government and we must differentiate from time to time the duties of local and national government. Many brilliant students of political economy feel that we have reached the point where the direction of our course must be determined. It would be an easy matter to adopt a mode of action that would set up a bureaucracy of a most deadening character, or equally simple to slip into a position from which we could not recover without reliving the struggles of the early American pioneers. One of the most significant political problems before our people today is that concerned with the work of the national government. To demand that it take a hand in local affairs is to invite the breakdown of our system of government. This we cannot afford. President Hoover has given much thought and attention to this phase of our political problems. His opinion merits the closest consideration on the part of every progressive citizen of our country.

"In Lincoln's day the dominant problem in our form of government turned upon the issue of States rights. Though less pregnant with disaster, the dominant problem today in our form of government turns in large degree upon the issue of the relationship of Federal, State, and local government responsibilities. We are faced with unceasing agitation that the Federal Government shall assume new financial burdens, that it shall undertake increased burdens in regulation of abuses and in the prosecution of crime.

"It is true that since Lincoln's time many forces have swept across State borders and have become more potent than the State or local community can deal with alone either financially or by jurisdiction. Our concept of Federal, State, and local responsibilities is possible of no unchangeable definitions and it must shift with the moving forces in the Nation, but the time has come when we must have more national consideration and decision of the part which each shall assume in these responsibilties.

"The Federal Government has assumed many new responsibilities since Lincoln's time, and will probably assume more in the future when the States and local communities can not alone cure abuse or bear the entire cost of national progress, but there is an essential principle that should be maintained in this matter. I am convinced that where Federal action is essential then in most cases it should limit its responsibilities to supplement the States and local communities, and that it should not assume the major rôle or the entire responsibility, in replacement of the States or local government, which is the very basis of self-government.

"The moment responsibilities of any community, particularly in economic and social questions, are shifted from any part of the Nation to Washington, then that community has subjected itself to a remote bureaucracy with its minimum of understanding and of sympathy. It has lost a large part of its voice and its control of its own destiny. Under Federal control the varied conditions of life in our country are forced into standard molds, with all their limitations upon life, either of the individual or the community. Where people divest themselves of local government responsibilities they at once lay the foundation for the destruction of their liberties.

"And buried in this problem lies something even deeper. The whole of our governmental machinery was devised for the purpose that through ordered liberty we give incentive and equality of opportunity to every individual to rise to that highest achievement of which he is capable. At once when government is centralized there arises a limitation upon the liberty of the individual and a restriction of individual opportunity. The true growth of the Nation is the growth of character in its citizens. The spread of government destroys initiative and thus destroys character. Character is made in the community as well as in the individual by assuming responsibilities, not by escape from them. Carried to its logical extreme, all this shouldering of individual and community responsibility upon the Government can lead but to the superstate where every man becomes the servant of the State and real liberty is lost. Such was not the government that Lincoln sought to build.

"There is an entirely different avenue by which we may both resist this drift to centralized government and at the same time meet a multitude of problems. That is to strengthen in the Nation a sense and an organization of self-help and cooperation to solve as many problems as possible outside of government."

In these paragraphs Mr. Hoover outlines two very definite functions of the national government.

In the first place, he believes that government must foster individual liberty among all the people by encouraging local and state authorities to assume their share of public responsibility. This method calls for a larger interest on the part of people in public affairs. In fact it creates interest in public problems. This spread of responsibility makes a government more flexible on the one hand and more effective on the other, because no man is called upon to bear burdens beyond the capacity of human knowledge and energy. A government that touches the lives of all the people through its local units is responsive as well as responsible. It reacts to the delicate processes of ordered liberty in every phase of life within its jurisdiction and in every geographical section within its limits. The overlapping of individual and group responsibility is readily recognized as one of the most significant problems which has grown out of the socializing processes of our civilization. The government, in practically every phase of local and national life, is over-reaching the boundaries of its natural jurisdiction. In some cases small communities assume the responsibility of the larger units, while in other cases the national government carries the burdens which rightly belong to local units. This condition compels the consideration of the problem of defining and classifying the function of political control. In times of prosperity public leaders often seek extension of power while in times of depression they ask relief from responsibility. Only the ideal of individualism can be made effective in this field since the general principle of local responsibility carried by local units offers the surest safeguard of personal liberty. At this time, we, like Mr. Hoover while Secretary of Commerce, must think more and more in terms of the classification of people. For if leaders become confused about their duties, civilization itself loses its way. Such an ideal guarantees individual freedom within the limits of official responsibility, and accordingly it prevents the cramping of individual effort.

In the second place, the executives should encourage individuals and organizations to "solve as many problems as possible outside of government." So far as the President is concerned this duty is extra-constitutional. This responsibility lies outside of the duties outlined for him by the constitution. It is in this field that our national executive can demonstrate administrative leadership. It is here that his personal ability is allowed freedom of expression. This is one of the standards by which executive leadership should be measured. And it may not be out of place to say parenthetically, that Mr. Hoover has assumed an unusual responsibility in this field. He is making a contribution that history will acclaim as one of the great achievements of his administration.

Perhaps the President's idea of extra-constitutional activity can best be shown by calling attention to the methods and management of many of our American colleges and universities. In many of these institutions a regular course of study called the curriculum is outlined by the faculty and closely followed by both students and teachers. The function of the college is believed to be that of using the course of study as a means to introduce the student without waste of energy through the trial and error method to the vital necessities of life. The curriculum usually determines the administrative methods and limits the executive activities of the officials of the college and at the same time definitely sets an upper and lower limit to the activities of the students. This limited program of mental activity which naturally includes the fundamentals of the general field of intellectual endeavor neither meets all of the needs of the student nor requires all of his time. Accordingly many so-called extra-curricular activities have claimed the interest of the average American student body. Many of these are considered by both the administrative officers and students to be quite as helpful and important as items in the regular curriculum. These extra-curricular enterprises have not only helped to socialize the entire college program but they have democratized the administrative methods and have enlarged the field of educational service. This state of affairs, in the main, has had the approval of men and women of vision and culture on the college staff because it has helped to create and hold the interest of a majority of students and it has placed responsibility upon all the individuals capable of accepting leadership.

America, then, with her college graduates in places of leadership and responsibility should be able to limit the activities of government to the irreducible minimum through constitutional limitation and at the same time carry forward a dynamic social program covering many enterprises of an extra-constitutional nature. Under the influence of this governmental ideal together with that of local control the individual freely develops qualities of self-restraint and self-reliance. He agrees with Cicero that "Excessive liberty leads both nations and individuals into excessive slavery," for when a government becomes too free in the exercise of power it begins to decline and whenever an individual becomes too free in the exercise of privilege he begins to enslave himself. He enjoys ordered liberty which is a natural outgrowth of democratic governmental procedure. It is inherent in the situation.

Let us turn now to a study of this function of government as it is related to another field of action other than that of free participation in government itself. If it is the function of government as Mr. Hoover has said, to guarantee liberty, it must be concerned with this in phases of life not related to state or national organizations.

Here in America we have won the intellectual and spiritual battle waged in defense of religious liberty. Our whole nation in no small measure owes its doctrine of liberty to the religious people who came to our shores under circumstances clouded with fear and suspicion. Out of these personal convictions grew the idea of a free people guided only by the dictates of an educated and spiritually sensitized conscience. President Hoover expressed appreciation of this historical background when in speaking of the ideal of self-government he declared: "No student of American history can fail to realize that these principles and ideals grew largely out of the religious origins and spiritual aspirations of our people."

Again, in discussing the ideal of equal opportunity in all the systems of government he observed that, "It is significant that some of these systems deny religion and seek to expel it. I can not conceive of a wholesome social order or a sound economic system that does not have its roots in religious faith. No blind materialism can for long engage the loyalties of mankind. Economic aspiration, though it strongly marks the American system, is not an end in itself, but is only one of many instruments to accomplish the profound purposes of the American people, which are largely religious in origin. This country is supremely dedicated, not to the pursuit of material riches, but to pursuit of a richer life for the individual."

Out of this concept of the function of government as determined by its spiritual origins, Mr. Hoover has developed a spirit of religious tolerance which he expresses in words that fire the imagination and challenge the unqualified support of men who cherish religious liberty and who know that it is the basis of social and governmental freedom.

In contrasting the statement of an early American minister of religion with his we have a mental measuring rod with which to determine the extension of the radius of our circle of personal liberty during the past three centuries. The minister declared:

"To say that men ought to have liberty of conscience is impious ignorance; religion admits of no eccentric notions."

"By blood and conviction," says Mr. Hoover, "I stand for religious tolerance both in act and in spirit. The glory of our American idealism is the right of every man to worship God according to the dictates of his own conscience."

DEMOCRATIC JUSTICE

When Mr. Hoover mentions justice as the second function of government he at once provokes inquiry into the nature of government itself. He compels an investigation of one of the central purposes of democracy. He brings into the focus of attention a problem which has claimed the interest of the best minds of all ages. In the twentieth century we face this problem either with the firm belief that democracy grants justice or with the question of the efficacy of this form of government in the adjustment of social inconsistencies.

There are those who claim that democracy can not be just because of its deliberate plan of action and because of its diffusion of responsibility. However, our American government has, in spite of all its possible weaknesses, demonstrated to the world at large that it has discovered the pivotal principle of social advancement. Justice can be experienced only under circumstances which permit every individual to seek it on the one hand and to resist injustice on the other. This thought is inherent in our American way of life and as an ideal it is an outgrowth of American Individualism.

Unless every member of a group has some responsibility in furthering justice and in combating injustice there can be no real justice. Mr. Hoover has this in mind as he attempts to throw all the weight of public opinion in favor of preserving our accomplishments in the realm of individual initiative and control. He appreciates the fact that ordered freedom which, as we have learned, involves both self-restraint and self-reliance, supports a theory of justice that demands both negative and positive governmental action.

Our legal code and jury system are maintained for purposes of control on the one hand and guidance on the other. As one acquaints himself with the history of legal jurisprudence he is confronted with the fact that law had its origin for the most part in a negative philosophy of life. Its main purpose was to serve as an agency of restraint while its controlling element was, "Thou shalt not." Such law throughout history has served to steady the human race, but it has appealed to the emotion of fear and used as its weapon of government the tool of punishment. Even though it has held the human race within the limits of social usage at times, it has hindered the social group by limiting individual initiative and effort. Autocratic governments have never been able to overcome this difficulty. They are not able to guarantee justice because they cannot allow the free participation of the individual in its promotion.

Governmental leaders who have depended upon negative law as a means of human control have failed to take into consideration a psychological law of prime importance. The structure of the human brain is so constituted as to make positive action easy. It naturally responds to a constructive program because it is dynamic in expression. Of course the nervous system is so organized as to permit the human body to retreat or withdraw in face of blocked activity. This action has sometimes been considered negative in nature whereas it is positive reaction to a negative cause or idea. In view of this psychological condition we learn that justice cannot be confined within the limits of restraining laws and personal punishment.

The government must place greater emphasis by far upon the central dynamic tendency of human action. Because of recent remarkable discoveries in the fields of juvenile research and investigation, unusual interest is being aroused in a program of individual guidance. With Mr. Hoover we have discovered that justice as a governmental quality is attained through all agencies, such as the home, the church, and the school, which assume responsibility for personal counseling. Justice of this character becomes synonymous with the best interests of all social processes. It is inherent in the growth and progress of the race. It includes every human quality that is in any way contributory to the growth of personality.

President Hoover has attempted to arouse the interest of the American people in this forward-looking and far-reaching interpretation of justice. He has stepped aside from the routine duties of his great office in order that he might give leadership to numerous enterprises which have the welfare of the people at heart. He has tried to think constructively with men and women upon whose shoulders rest the responsibility of furnishing leadership in this comparatively new field of social effort. In this course of action, he has the support of progressive thinkers throughout our country. Those who agree with him have learned that life creates life, while law regulates it. They recognize, therefore, that justice is as much concerned with the growth of people as it is with the interpretation and application of law. They understand that the law, which is the condensed common sense of the ages, has ever kept the jury or committee from being too lenient while the jury or committee has kept the law from being too violent. This interaction between the law and the person or persons who acts as the court and the individual who appears before the court gives opportunity for both the personal and historical element to enter decisions which are made in the name of justice.

Now justice does not originate in the government. It has its beginning in people who live justly and who, in their attempt to live justly use the government which they themselves have set up to give expression to this the greatest of human qualities.

A just man is one who has developed an evenly balanced personality. He is able to intellectualize his experience, moralize his intellect, inspirationalize his morals, and functionalize his inspiration. These co-extensive mental reactions are of equal value. This type of mental response and the growth of spiritual personality are co-expansive.

A just person analyzes and synthesizes his experience in order that future action might result in practical achievement. If decisions which concern the lives of others are made without reference to either real or vicarious experience, they might carry seriously unjust implications. Decisions of this kind are apt to lack the warmth of human interest. When a sufficient number of individuals in a nation interpret a sufficient number of experiences they develop a mental attitude. Collectively they intellectualize experience.

When the just man has considered his experience often enough and clearly enough, he begins to draw definite conclusions. These conclusions he builds into an ethical code and by so doing he moralizes his intellect. He becomes concerned with the establishment of moral norms or standards which finally take the form of laws or proverbs. Very early in the history of mankind the need of such norms was discovered. Mental, moral, and spiritual economy demanded their establishment and acceptance. These soon became the simplest and easiest methods by which experience was transmitted from one generation to the next.

When it became necessary for the first great social and spiritual leader to direct the conduct of his associates, in his attempt to be just he turned aside to secure for them those ten immortal laws called the Commandments. They have served as guideposts throughout the centuries, keeping unnumbered thousands upon the pathway of honesty, integrity, and sobriety. Some have found in them the voice of God; others have found in them the voice of humanity; some others have found in them both the voice of God and the voice of humanity; while still others have found in them neither the voice of God nor the voice of humanity. To the latter group the probability of the moralization of the intellect is negligible because all law is considered an instrument of control only as it relates to the lives of others. There is little personal interest in it. People with such a negative legal philosophy cannot appreciate the importance and significance of the words of Samuel Johnson when he says, "The law is the last result of human wisdom acting upon human experience for the benefit of the public."

The just man inspirationalizes these rules of conduct. His obedience to law is the result of inward impulsion rather than outward compulsion. He reduces all social law to one or more dynamic personal principles. He understands the value of translating negative law which he has inherited from the historic past into positive postulates. By so doing, he, as an individual, inspirationalizes the moral code of his day and when a sufficient number of people respond in this way a spiritual upthrust takes place in human society.

The just man as a member of this group is now prepared to functionalize his inspiration. He is ready to go to work. But how shall he value the work which he is to do? The mere fact of his interest in it cannot prevent fanaticism on the one hand nor wasted effort on the other. Work that is satisfactory to him must provide for free mental and physical responses that expand experience, improve intellect, and stabilize morals. Personal poise and dignity are developed through work that has a social as well as an individual value. Functionalized inspiration, then, makes possible purposeful activity which prevents intellectual incompetency, moral mediocrity, and social inferiority. It stimulates mental achievement, moral mastery, and spiritual ascendency, all of which find expression in social justice.

The government is charged with the responsibility of providing social agencies which create just persons. Then too, it must maintain institutions in which to care for those who cannot or will not be just. Its main task in this connection is that of arranging a national and local environment through the encouragement of moral and spiritual institutions that will influence the individual to live a just life.

President Hoover is moved by this sense of justice. Experience has convinced him that civilization makes lasting progress through the growth and development of the individual. He knows that without this objective, government is apt to consider property rights above human rights.

INTELLECTUAL WELFARE

The third function of government as the need of the individual is considered, covers the general field of intellectual welfare. Mr. Hoover lists this as the third objective even though he would not rank it third in importance. In keeping with his theory of local government he believes that this is primarily the function of the state. In this belief he has the support of the United States Constitution which did not allude to the subject of education either directly or indirectly unless perhaps it was included in the list of duties not mentioned in Article Ten under the Amendments—duties which were specifically left to the consideration and the control of the state.

"The creation of an official system of universal and free education," says he, "with its progress stage by stage from the lowest grade in our public schools to the highest training in our universities and colleges has thus become a primary responsibility of every state. It is the right of every youth in the state."

In this statement two very definite points of view are outlined. He supports a theory that has worked remarkably well in the realm of public education ever since the adoption of the constitution. One of the great safeguards against a too centralized form of government is the state-controlled educational program. Training in the public schools in the commonwealths of our republic has for the most part included a course in the history of the state in which the child was born and reared. Such training furnished the local patriotic background and limited and colored the vision of our citizenry. No single provision in the constitution either positive or negative is wiser than this arrangement. Under this method the national government cannot easily educate and train the individual to believe that he is only its subject. It has a tendency to teach the significance of our American Individualism in that the government was made for man and not man for the government, the same as the Sabbath was made for man and not man for the Sabbath. Nothing is more definitely American than this particular governmental theory even though it is hard for the most progressive and learned people not thoroughly familiar with our historical background to understand and appreciate.

Mr. Hoover's second proposal in the foregoing statement clearly points out the significance of this suggestion. It is the right of every youth in the state, not because he is a subject of the state, but because he is a citizen with all the rights and privileges which that term connotes. As a theory of government we have always believed in the value of the common man, in the sacredness of personality, and the inalienable rights of individuality. Education under this progressive governmental ideal is not a means to an end, it is an end in itself just as the end or aim of life is life itself. The theory that a person is educated for the state contradicts the principles of individualism which brought the early pioneers to this country and encouraged them in their program of school and church building. To be educated for the state means that the state has a right to use the individual as a means to an end, even though the use to which he is put is detrimental to him, which is one and the same as believing that a certain group of people in authority for a limited period of time has the right to control and use people who through the ballot gave them that authority and power. When Mr. Hoover says that it is the right of every youth in the state to have an education he simply means that adult society owes to the growing generation intellectual privileges equal or superior to those they themselves enjoyed as gifts of the preceding generation. He would not have an individual used by the state for either immediate or remote ends if such use brought inconvenience and discomfort to the one being used. Only in times of national crises would he submit to such an exigency. No plan of procedure will safeguard this fundamental American ideal to a greater extent than state and county control of education. It becomes the duty of the national government to encourage and support in every possible way the work undertaken by the various states in the union. It is not its duty to control the system of education in detail. To do so would destroy the foundations of democracy. Such a theory of education is in keeping with the idea of the intrinsic value of the individual. This does not mean that the individual has no state nor national responsibility. It means just the opposite. Under one system he may be forced to do that which his conscience demands he shall not do. Under the other he assumes the responsibility of citizenship with a free and open mind. He is a cooperative citizen not a ward of the state.

William Penn once said, "If men be good government cannot be bad." Mr. Hoover says:

"Law can not rise above its source in good citizenship—in what right-minded men most earnestly believe and desire. If the law is upheld only by government officials, then all law is at an end. . . . The orderly administration of the law involves more than the mere machinery of law enforcement. The efficent use of that machinery and a spirit in our people in support of law are alike essential."

With this general principle either consciously or unconsciously the American people agree. For upon this theory we have built a system of education which has as its purpose the training of every child for citizenship in our republic. Since the days of Horace Mann we have believed in the improvability of the human race through education. We have always had confidence in the efficacy of moral and intellectual training and have arranged our annual community budgets so as to provide schools in order that our children might have every opportunity to grow into normal members of modern society.

Two considerations however, sometimes provoke inquiry on the part of the far-sighted citizen interested primarily in the processes of character building. The very fact that we train for citizenship in the city, county, state, and nation makes the close observer of our educational procedure question the interest which the administrator and the teacher take in the individual child or prospective citizen. Then too, when national reports show the enormous size of our local school projects, the inquirer is led to ask concerning the amount of individual attention each child receives and at once the citizen and the educator agree that the principle of American Individualism cannot succeed as a basis of democratic government until it has worked in the field of education. Anyone familiar with the development and progress of American civilization is impressed with the close coordination of these two phases of public life.

The state capitol building which usually houses the office of the state superintendent of public instruction, and the county courthouse which includes in its list of county offices that of county superintendent of schools is sufficient evidence of the interlocking of these two great public interests. These permanent physical arrangements clearly indicate the ideas and ideals of the builders of our country.

The system of education, during a period of approximately three hundred years, has served the state faithfully and well. This has been true because control in matters of finance and employment rested in the hands of a school board consisting of laymen. Should anyone doubt that the school was conducted for the state, let him study the oaths that teachers from time to time have been required to take, and in addition let him review the subject matter of the course of study required of every child. There was a time when only one side of large and important issues was presented to the pupil and that side was of course always favorable to the best interest of our government. Other methods and attitudes could not have been sanctioned by public thought because we had not yet reached the period of scientific analysis and interpretation. But during the past half century a new philosophy of education has gradually but certainly developed. The attitude toward individual heroes in public life and toward methods and policies in government began to change with the introduction of the scientific method of studying and writing history. The older attitude was one of conserving and protecting individual and group interests while the newer is one of finding and interpreting the facts regardless of their personal or social implications. It is altogether likely that some of our modern scholars have gone too far into the realm of destructive criticism, but on the whole, the past quarter of a century has experienced a wholesome change in educational outlook.

It is true that even today many schools are maintained by the church and by the government with the specific aim of training students for service within the respective organizations. The church has at times educated the individual for the church while the government has educated him for the government. The major interest and purpose of such education is of course, the welfare and progress of the organization rather than the development of the individual. Such institutions were, and are, known as organization centered schools. Under these conditions the individual is trained to be used as a means to an end, the end being service under the direction and authority of a group. While individual initiative and effort are allowed in varying degrees, within rather well-defined limits, on the whole, personality is largely motivated and controlled from without rather than from within.

But this is not the ideal of the great American public school. It is an individual-centered institution. Its aim and purpose is that of assisting the child in his efforts to live a satisfactory life. It seeks to help prepare him to do effectively and well that which he has chosen to do or that which he will choose to do as a unit of a social order.

Now the government, both state and national, should be vitally concerned with a program of education that prepares individuals to function successfully in the business and industrial world. It is well for us to be reminded from time to time of the contribution that our system of education is making in this particular field. We must not overlook the fact that departments and schools of business administration in our colleges and universities have grown with startling rapidity during the past quarter of a century. For the most part these institutions have focused upon the task of educating and training leaders in the field of business. These leaders have become somewhat acquainted in their general college course with the social and philosophic ideals of our civilization. After completing this course in the school of business administration many of them, at once, go to places of responsibility in the economic world. Under the urge of this necessity, well rounded courses in psychology, sociology, and philosophy have been required of the students in these schools. They have been trained in an environment which places the highest value upon people rather than upon administrative methods and factory tools. Accordingly they give means rather than numbers to their men. They not only pay wages sufficiently high to guarantee a respectable living for the worker and his family, but they even share profits with the men who do the mechanical work. Their highest objective aside from serving the community with the objects they handle and the contributions they make out of their own profits is that of creating an environment in which the workers can find daily satisfaction in their work—satisfaction which comes through personal achievement. Deans and directors of these schools have recognized the fundamental necessity of high ethical standards and ideals of social helpfulness.

But it would be utterly useless for our independent and state controlled colleges to train leaders of this character without giving the same consideration to people who are to be their associates in the great business and industrial enterprises of our country. The less education given the slave, the more apt he was to serve the master without complaint and dissatisfaction. But in a democratic social order the more the worker has the more apt he is to function as a unit in a corporate body. Accordingly our system of public education introduces the child in the modern progressive kindergarten to a social program that leads eventually through the elementary grades into the field of industry and commerce. The school boy of today is the workman of tomorrow. While in the public schools enjoying the satisfaction of social privilege and achievement he is only a few years removed from economic responsibility. Now the school that trains the child for a job serves well the government which uses the man as a means to an end. The school that educates the child for a place of social responsibility and economic independence serves well the government which considers the individual of intrinsic value and of social importance. Either of these points of view may be built into the philosophy of our government within a very short time.

It is interesting to note that during the period of economic depression which began late in 1929 few, if any, disturbances of a major order occurred. President Hoover in speaking before a group of people interested in economic problems called attention to the fact that less than three hundred strikes had occurred as compared with twenty-two hundred in a previous crisis. That the public schools made this contribution to American civilization can hardly be doubted even though it is often overlooked by students of economic progress.

We should discover, if we can, the causes which hold steady our people and give stability to our government under such times of economic strain. For it is during these periods that people everywhere prophesy the possibility of outbreaks ruthless in character and detrimental in results. Only those who understand the steadying influence of the compelling ideal of American Individualism can appreciate the real reasons for the courage and fortitude and common sense of the great mass of American citizens during times of such distress. The reasons are to be found in the American system of public instruction.

Too often candidates for public office, reporters for political journals and students of governmental procedure fail to take into account trends in the field of education. They appear to be unaware of the fact that it takes only a comparatively short time to change political policies after new biological and psychological laws are discovered. But the importance of being acquainted with the findings and beliefs of the educators of a given period is easily observable when attention is given school statistics.

In order to prepare either a man or woman to serve the public in capacity of teacher, the state has outlined some rather definite educational requirements. Two of these from a governmental point of view are of supreme importance. They give content and direction to our common thought. They are shaping the destiny of our nation. The first has to do with classroom or pupil management (a course in administration), and the second with an understanding of the nature, growth, and adjustment of the child (a course in psychology).

When the state, through its department of education, requires the training schools and colleges to teach its prospective teachers how to manage or direct the activities of children, it at the same time strengthens the foundations of democratic government.

This problem of control or pupil management has been a question of scientific research since the beginning of the formal study of educational technique just as the problem of adult control has been a question of scientific investigation since the beginning of the formal study of political economy. Departments and schools of education of our colleges and universities have changed the attitude of our American public on this question and in turn they have paved the way for a new and more reasonable system of control in governmental affairs. City, county, and state superintendents of public instruction who have been trained in these institutions are now serving as executives of school systems where teachers of like training are serving. Together they are carrying the most advanced principles of educational procedure in the realm of discipline to the remote sections of our republic. They are controlling children by the use of modern methods which often makes the technique used by officers of the law in the same community as they attempt to control the same children, either during their school or post-school experience, seem altogether unjust and inequitable. Such a condition at once shows the necessity of proper technical training on the part of all public officials because in the final analysis control in adult life must naturally grow out of the methods used in the control of children. Such reasoning has led experts in the field of education to believe that if corporal punishment is a useless method in dealing with adults, it is obviously needless in dealing with children.

Methods of discipline and control based upon punishment, of course, are rigid in application but negative in result. However, it cannot be denied that control by these methods is economical so far as the expenditure of moral and intellectual vigor is concerned. It requires little time, scarcely any patience, and certainly no thought. In fact it can easily become quite automatic. It may after a time be turned over without much inconvenience to the force of habit.

Perhaps it can now be said without much fear of contradiction that teachers who use such methods are more interested in lessons than they are in children. The school to such instructors is much the same as the government is to politicians. It must be kept while the government must be run. The purpose of such a school is to learn lessons and recite them, while the purpose of such a government is to collect revenue and spend it. A cursory survey of history seems to indicate that the lesson-centered school and the revenue-centered government have been contemporary institutions. The human element in each, if not entirely lacking, is reduced to a point almost beyond recognition. Certainly there is little appreciation of the intrinsic value of individual personality. These autocratic methods in education pave the way for similar methods in government.

At the opening session of the White House Conference on Child Health and Protection, President Hoover expressed a convincing opinion when he said:

"From your explorations into the mental and moral endowment and opportunities of children will develop new methods to inspire their creative work and play, to substitute love and self-discipline for the rigors of rule, to guide their recreations into wholesome channels, to steer them past the reefs of temptation, to develop their characters, and to bring them to adult age in tune with life, strong in moral fiber, and prepared to play more happily their part in the productive tasks of human society."

A school motivated by such a philosophy of education makes the child the center of every physical and intellectual activity. It individualizes him because of the democratic methods and controls used in his education.

If education lays the foundation of an impersonal philosophy of life by considering the child as a means to an end rather than an end in himself, the government which quickly comes under the control of these same children will probably use the individual for selfish governmental purposes. It at once becomes plain that love cannot be the law of the school and hatred the law of the government. Perhaps no man in American political life, because of experience and training, more thoroughly appreciates this state of affairs than President Hoover. His entire educational background had in it the elements of friendly understanding and helpful appreciation. He thinks and speaks the language of modern education.

If Mr. Hoover is correct in the statement that "national character cannot be built by law," the modern educator must be right when he says that national character can be built through shared experience—cordial interaction between mature teachers and immature students. Character always takes form under the compelling influence of a helpful personality. Friendship is the educational medium through which it is achieved. But the question might arise concerning the power or efficacy of the law of friendship as applied to the problem of restoring delinquent children, which if not solved, eventually becomes one of reclaiming mal-adjusted adults. During the past few years the state of California has been carrying forward one of the most remarkable experiments in the history of American juvenile control. At the state school in Los Angeles County where on an average there are more than three hundred boys registered, a program of re-education or rehabilitation is under way. These boys have all been taken from their homes and their communities because of maladjustment. Some unsocial act made it necessary for the judicial authorities to institutionalize them. They represent every religious creed, every race, every type of home condition, and every type of mental ability. The rule is that corporal punishment cannot be used as a means of direction and discipline. The authorities agree with Mr. Hoover that "We need to turn the methods of inquiry from the punishment of delinquency to the causes of delinquency. It is not the delinquent child that is at the bar of judgment, but society itself."

A visit to the school readily convinces the visitor that corporal punishment and consequent fear are out of harmony with the friendly ideals of the administration. Two principles of control are easily contrasted in the mind of the observer. First, where corporal punishment is used, there is an attempt to control conduct through stimulation of the emotion of fear. Second, where rewards are used there is an attempt to direct conduct through stimulation of the emotion of respect or admiration. It is worthy of note that everywhere criminologists, jurists, ministers, psychologists, and educators are beginning to place proper value upon the law of respect even when dealing with delinquents and criminals. The first method, that of punishment, has been tried as a means of social control throughout the centuries, yet little if any, progress has been made in the science of dealing with unsocial individuals when this method is in common use. Progressive leaders everywhere believe that it is time now to try the second method, or at least coordinate these two.

For the past fifty years American education has been definitely and persistently driving toward control by means of the law of reward rather than the law of punishment. This change in the administrative point of view in the system of education has led to a positive and constructive change in the point of view concerning control of peoples and nations, particularly those considered wards or dependencies of the larger nations. Common sense has supplanted the emotion of fear and if executive and administrative public officials want to succeed in this generation they must now begin to adjust their methods of control in government to the methods of control in education. Mr. Hoover is taking account of this national situation in his effort to share the responsibility with people everywhere.

The second fundamental requirement made by the state upon the teacher is that he shall have at least some psychological knowledge of the growth and development of the child. The state, in outlining its system of education, has recognized the fact that the successful teacher is one who thoroughly understands the child's original nature or his inherited tendencies. Without such knowledge his efforts to help the child adjust himself to modern society would be of little or no value. Having acknowledged this necessity in the field of education the state has assumed that whatever social processes favor child development at the same time function in national and finally in international affairs.

Leaders primarily interested in the welfare of humanity are now even willing to test the validity of government itself by the fundamental laws of human nature. In our country we have consistently held the theory that the individual could be trusted as a unit of the larger group. We have believed that by nature he is constructive rather than destructive. Democracy must stand or fall on this modern American ideal. The validity of the democratic ideal in government, if our highest opinion of the individual is correct, is determined by the inherent nature of our people. In view of the widespread discussion of the philosophy of American Individualism, which in turn supports our democratic government, it will be possible for us here to put our government to this test. The value of a government and the methods used by it must be determined by the validity of the principles which hold any group of people together as a unit and which serve to direct the adaptive processes of life. If we are to show the validity of the democratic ideal we must defend the thesis that democracy is a creative social force. Two questions of far reaching importance arise:

Is democracy in keeping with the fundamental physiological law of evolution or progress?

Is it in keeping with the fundamental psychological law of human development?

In answering these questions we assume of course,

that we are interested in a democracy of liberty which results in an uplifting social process rather than a democracy of equality which results in a levelling process which tends to produce mediocrity. A democracy of liberty tends to develop individual initiative and responsibility both of which are essential to progress, while a democracy of equality tends to foster mass movements or group action often devoid of intelligent leadership. A democracy of liberty is, according to students of the constitution, exactly what the writers of that document had in mind when they discussed equality. With this definition in mind, let us attempt an answer to the foregoing questions. Autocracy is based on the theory of a survival of the fittest in physiological evolution, but according to modern biologists it has a false basis for its assumption. This point of view is clearly set forth and the answer to our first question suggested by Professor Eugene Lyman of New York, who is one of our leading philosophic thinkers:

"The struggle for existence is not the chief source of progress, even in the lower orders of life. What it does is to preserve the fittest and so to establish a species after it has been formed. But progress arises from variation, and spontaneous production of more advantageous characteristics. Now in the social realm democracy gives far wider range to the possibilities of variation than aristocracy. Moreover, in the highest ranges of evolution the competition or struggle for existence is between ideals, methods and institutions, and does not necessarily involve elimination or subordination of persons at all. As for altruism being a hindrance to progress because it preserves the unfit, the effort to redeem all human life is one of the chief sources of the science through which the laws of physical and social hygiene are discovered. And further, this effort bears fruit in sympathy and appreciation of personality, without which *social* progress would soon cease. What altruism may do is to eliminate the conditions that produce handicapped men. But to eliminate the handicapped men themselves or to abandon them to their fate, would undermine the social solidarity without which no real progress of the race is thinkable."

The answer to the second question is to be found in a further quotation from the same author:

"Democracy is optimistic in a sense that autocracy cannot be, because it believes in such a development and organization of society as shall make the whole human race sharers, not only in the enjoyment, but in the production, of culture.

"And thereby it overcomes the great inconsistencies of autocracy. It excludes the possibility of the welfare of a caste or class rivalling the welfare of the race; and it does not call on those, who at present are unprivileged, to be content with admiring and honoring a culture in the producing and enjoying of which they can have no share. And so far as eugenics is seen to enter into progress, there is no reason why that doctrine should not be incorporated into democracy. Moreover, the Will to Service is not empty of content, as is the Will to Power. For service takes into account all human interests and needs as such, instead of justifying men in brushing aside whatever may stand in the way of the exercise of power."

We may assume then that the democratic ideal is valid as a basis of governmental theory in that it is in harmony with the physiological law of evolution, namely "differentiation of function," and that it is in harmony with the psychological law of human progress in that it tends to produce an optimistic spirit on the part of the masses, which, in turn, is a prerequisite to spiritual, intellectual, and social advancement.

It is in light of such thoughts as these that our individualistic way of life in America raises itself to the highest possible point of satisfaction and service.

At no point in our civilization do our democratic forces reach a higher level of perfection than in our public schools. The state is right in emphasizing the necessity of teaching teachers to know and understand the growth and development of the individual child, for out of such a study comes an appreciation of democratic government itself. Through sharing experience with democratic teachers children themselves have the opportunity of growing into democratic citizens capable of understanding the biological and psychological laws of human advancement for "our teachers more than any other group," says President Hoover, "have both the privilege and the duty to guide the steps of each new generation on the road of democracy."

All that we have been saying about education finally leads to a consideration of leadership, a most important item in democracy. As a matter of fact education not only provides leadership, but it protects democracy itself by providing men and women capable of assuming social responsibility. "By building this open stair we set up a fundamental protection to our democracy itself, for it is the maintenance of leadership by the rise of the individual out of the mass which assures us against the crystallization of classes or special groups. No stratification or segregation of classes or castes can take place in a mass livened by the free stir of its particles."

In the following sentences Mr. Hoover outlines the conditions under which leadership in American public life can be advanced:

"Our leadership can be found and it will be sympathetic to our ideals if we maintain the decency and dignity of family life through a stable economic system; if we maintain free and universal education and thus provide them the open stair to leadership. If we maintain for every individual an equality of opportunity to attain that position in the community to which his character and his ability entitle him. Then our supply of leadership will stream forward of its own impulse. It is in this insistence upon an equal chance and a free road to rise in leadership that our great American experiment has departed from those of history. It is our sure guarantee of the future. In its vast possibilities is the hope of every mother for her boys and her girls. Under such leadership, replenished constantly from the great mass of our people, we can aspire to a democracy which will express a common purpose for the common good. We can build a civilization where national conscience is alert to protect the rights of all, curtail selfish economic power, and hold to the ideal of distributed contentment among the whole people."

We learn from these words that education plays a large part in our national life by producing trained leadership. These leaders in turn foster and support the program of education and as this socializing process continues generation after generation the intellectual welfare of the people is promoted by and through the government.

EQUALITY OF OPPORTUNITY

The fourth privilege which the government assures to the individual according to Mr. Hoover is that of equality of opportunity. No subject is mentioned more frequently nor with greater emphasis in his writings than this. It is the central theme of his system of political economy. The two institutions most responsible for the development of a community situation in which equality of opportunity might be enjoyed by every American child are the home and the school. One of the real tests of democratic government as he sees it is its interest in the welfare of the home.

"The unit of American life," he declares, "is the family and the home. It is the economic unit as well as the moral and spiritual unit. But it is more than this. It is the beginning of self-government. It is the throne of our highest ideals. It is the source of the spiritual energy of our people. For the perfecting of this unit of national life we must bend all of our material and scientific ingenuity. For the attainment of this end we must lend every energy of the government.

"I have before emphasized that the test of our government is what it does to insure that the home is secure in material benefit and comfort; what it does to keep that home free from bureaucratic domination; what it does to open the door of opportunity to every boy and girl within it; what it does in building moral safeguards and strengthening moral and spiritual inspiration. From the homes of America must emanate that purity of inspiration only as a result of which we can succeed in self-government. I speak of this as a basic principle that should guide our national life. I speak of it as the living action of government in the building of a nation. I speak of it as the source from which government must rise to higher and higher standards of perfection from year to year."

One cannot contemplate the significance of these words and the ideas which they convey without believing that Mr. Hoover thoroughly understands the simple yet profound truth that the government of a democratic people cannot rise beyond the heights of their home life.

To supplement the work of the home in supporting the ideals which make for democratic progress we have conceived and built a system of public education. We have already discussed its task in this sphere of public enterprise under the title of intellectual welfare, but we must let Mr. Hoover evaluate the school as a social agency in the field of equal opportunity.

"It is absolutely essential to the moral development and the enlarged opportunity of the boys and girls in every home that we increasingly strengthen our public school system and our institutions of higher learning. . . . The first step to maintained equality of opportunity amongst our people is, as I have said before, that there should be no child in America who has not been born, and who does not live, under sound conditions of health; who does not have full opportunity for education from the kindergarten to the university; who is not free from injurious labor; who does not have stimulation to ambition to the fullest of his or her capacities. It is a matter of concern to our government that we should strength the safeguards to health. These activities of helpfulness and of co-operation stretch before us in every direction. A single generation of Americans of such a production would prevent more of crime and of illness, and give more of spirit and of progress than all of the repressive laws and police we can ever invent—and it would cost less."

STIMULATION TO SERVICE

With such a clear conception of governmental responsibility functioning through a program of universal education it is quite natural that Mr. Hoover would almost intuitively list stimulation to service as the fifth individualistic objective of government. It is this item in his list of governmental functions that socializes or spiritualizes his idea of American Individualism. Without this final ideal as a balancing factor, government growing out of an individualistic philosophy of life would indeed have a tendency to produce a social order the commanding characteristics of which would be avarice and greed.

We have already discussed some of the implications of the philosophy of service. We must now enquire concerning some of the organizations through which these principles might become applicable in human affairs.

Students of modern social problems conclude after careful study and research that out of experience grows thought and out of thought attitudes and out of attitudes philosophy and out of philosophy organization and out of organization civilization. To say it another way—civilization consists of organizations which give it direction and meaning; the organizations in turn are shaped and limited by the philosophy which brought them into being; philosophy then, is reduced to the attitudes which support and make possible well defined principles; attitudes are traced back to specific mental reactions called thoughts and thoughts are traced to real or imaginary experiences either simple or complex in nature and character. Experience then becomes the "ultimate universe of discourse" in the realm of social living.

In almost any growing or expanding process problems are solved by the trial and error method—or shall we say by the trial and success method—until sufficient evidence has accumulated through experience to justify the formulation of flexible rules. These rules in turn serve to direct others along the highway of life without the waste involved in the trial and error method provided, however, that they have the moral sanction of institutions of a high character. In this manner society becomes stable but not static.

Perhaps at no time in the history of the world has any civilization witnessed the development of organizations through which a constructive and forceful philosophy of service could express itself comparable to the first thirty years of the century in which we now live. Since the close of the World War associations whose prime object is that of mutual helpfulness have developed with amazing rapidity. Business, professional, and industrial leaders representing every vocation have banded together for the purpose of promoting this new idealism. While these clubs have many points in common with the secret fraternities of the past century, they have taken at least one advanced step. Even though their membership may be limited to a congenial group of men their desire to help is usually community wide in scope. Their meetings are open and visitors are always welcome, and their activities are limited only

by the extent of the need of a neighborhood. This
spirit of social helpfulness has spread until most of
the centers of population have one or more units.
Members have developed the custom of using the
full name in addressing each other, thus classifying
the individual and at the same time socializing him.
Suspicion has given place to confidence, criticism to
comradeship and rivalry to helpfulness. These
organizations and associations have adopted slogans
and outlined a code of ethics equal in importance for
this day to the Ten Commandments in early Hebrew
history. Accordingly President Hoover with a message for a new day and ideals for a new citizenship
could not have assumed leadership of the American
people at a moment in history so surcharged with an
idealistic philosophy in keeping with his own
thoughts and principles as at this hour. An analysis
of the code of ethics underlying these organizations
reveals a similar if not identical friendly idealism to
that which through the years he has tried to make
effective. He mentions these clubs in complimentary
terms when he makes the following observation:

"The vast multiplication of voluntary organizations for altruistic purposes are themselves proof of
the ferment of spirituality, service, and mutual responsibility. These associations for advancement of
public welfare, improvement, morals, charity, public
opinion, health, the clubs and societies for recreation
and intellectual advancement, represent something
moving at a far greater depth than 'joining.' They
represent the widespread aspiration for mutual ad-

vancement, self-expression, and neighborly helpfulness."

If members of these organizations accept with any degree of seriousness the central theme around which their organizations are built they cannot fail to mobilize public sentiment in favor of a spirit of friendship and comradeship. They have undertaken a piece of constructive work which is in harmony with their slogans and their codes of ethics. To strive to attain such a goal places behind the government of the United States a group of men who guarantee the creation of an idealism which throws about the individual equal opportunity and freedom.

If now we have in mind the significance of the five-fold purpose of government which Mr. Hoover so clearly follows we are ready to investigate the result of such a governmental program. We are reasonably certain that service could take no other than fifth place in the category of the functions of government because without the support of liberty, justice, education and opportunity, it would not carry such broad and comprehensive implications as it does. In analyzing service with its roots deep in the principle of sympathy we find it productive of security. Everywhere people are recognizing that without safety in society contentment is lacking. The words, liberty, justice, intelligence, opportunity, service, suggest the possibility of attaining a social and political order in which contentment finds general expression by virtue of the fact that there are contributing elements in the program of mutual understanding. If without security contentment is lacking, certainly without these five functions of society security cannot be expected, much less guaranteed. Security establishes a goal to be attained while the functions of government deal with a method of approach. Whenever the safety of a people is in jeopardy, progress is impossible. Society becomes stagnant. Progressive and constructive activities during the World War were at times sacrificed to the disintegrating processes of the conflict in which we were engaged. It was learned that without a feeling of security the mind cannot concentrate except upon the problem of security itself. It would not if it could. Security then, is a condition under which individual growth and social progress take place.

Our democracy through its functions of government has attempted to create a national situation favoring methods calculated to lead to this result. But democracy cannot, because of its inherent nature, guarantee fast or static security. If it did it would destroy the fundamental functions of government itself and by so doing rob the individual of its inherent social rights. Security to us today does not mean, as it has in the past, a protected position in the realm of economics, religion, or politics. But it does mean that every man shall be secure in his right to grow in each of these fields of human endeavor. This being true, service itself is the greatest guarantee of security. Church doctrine and theological creeds no longer guarantee security in religion; investment in gilt-edged securities no longer guarantees security in economics; a large and powerful army no longer guarantees security in government. Security in a growing and expanding world has always been found in the realm of social considerations. Sympathy compels service and service guarantees security. The man in public life today who receives commendation and support on the part of the public is usually the individual who has the largest capacity for service. This holds true in every phase of industrial and political life. If modern democracy carries any challenge of value and worth to the individual who enjoys liberty, justice, education, and opportunity because of governmental solicitude, it is this: that he shall in recognition of his privileges extend sympathy and render service, for in so doing he shall win security—a security that is the product of *cooperative individualism.*

Here our government faces its two most difficult problems. If in times of depression democratic governmental policies must be abandoned in order that people may be fed and if in times of national danger they must be discarded in order that people may be protected, the end of this form of government is in sight.

Indeed some of our people would, it seems, admit that in face of these problems democracy should provide for a temporary suspension of its policies because of the exigencies of a given situation. But such an attitude has supported the opponents of democracy in their contention that autocracy or bureaucracy furnish a superior form of government because they do not have to allow for even temporary suspension. To this argument the people of America will finally give answer by removing the causes of these problems. Neither kings nor governmental bureaus have brought about the elimination of economic dislocation nor the discontinuance of international conflict. This work must be done by the people through democratic methods under the inspiration of lofty ideals. During the past decade people have come to believe that the solutions of these problems are within the realm of human possibility. Certainly we are beginning to recognize them as a collective responsibility.

We turn then to a discussion of the problem of economics in the following chapter, and of war in the last, because we cannot carry the idea of American Individualism further unless it functions in face of difficulties involved in these realms of human experience.

CHAPTER IV

American Individualism and Economic Progress

Normal Realms of Economic Activity. Democratic Assistance and Control. Economic Freedom. Popular Responsibility.

"Our Government's greatest troubles and failures are in the economic field. Forty years ago the contact of the individual with the Government had its largest expression in the sheriff or policeman, and in debates over political equality. In those happy days the Government offered but small interference with the economic life of the citizen. But with the vast development of industry and the train of regulating functions of the national and municipal government that followed from it; with the recent vast increase in taxation due to the war;—the Government has become through its relations to economic life the most potent force for maintenance or destruction of our American individualism."

H. H.

CHAPTER IV

American Individualism and Economic Progress

EVEN though our American idea of progress is not confined to the realm of economic development, nevertheless this is one of the important phases of our national growth. It is a problem with which every student of government must deal if he is to appreciate the forces that have shaped American life. It is in this realm of human action that the individual needs the guidance and support of definite philosophic principles. Just as organic sensations furnish the foundation for mental and moral reactions, so economic conditions furnish the basis of social and political experience.

NORMAL REALMS OF ECONOMIC ACTIVITY

As a people we have experienced three phases of economic expansion distinguished by the terms, necessity, convenience, and luxury. Some of us have settled permanently in one of these three realms either because of our own wishes or circumstances beyond our control. As a matter of fact, growth of our civilization as a whole has developed along these lines. The pioneers who came from countries across the sea to the Eastern seaboard of our country lived for a great many years under conditions which provided the bare necessities of life. Their homes were constructed out of material which was provided by workmen using tools of the simplest design. The methods of lighting and heating were simple and inexpensive. Their churches and schools, built and equipped under the pressing demands of necessity were neither artistic nor comfortable. Their storehouses and places of business were crude and inconvenient. Their roads were mere paths leading from one community center to another, marked only by wayside objects of interest to the traveler. This indeed was a period characterized in all its phases by sheer necessity.

Then came the period of convenience. Creative thought and effort directed toward the solution of the problem of making lighter the burdens of ordinary living resulted in the invention and manufacture of devices which conserve energy. Homes, schools, and churches became more convenient because they were more safely and artistically constructed and equipped. Paths became roads under the care and direction of experienced highway builders, thus making travel easier and less hazardous. However, the art of living under these conditions, while relieved of much of the drudgery of the period of necessity, often involved a large amount of labor because many of the tools by means of which a living was produced were so designed as to demand the use of heavy manual labor in their operation.

Passing from this period of convenience our civilization moved into the third, which is one of luxury.

The pioneer sod house or log cabin has given place to the luxurious six- to ten-room dwelling of today with all its modern equipment and appliances. The one-room church building has given place to the luxurious religious education plant with departments for every division of the denomination. The one-unit schoolhouse has given place to the most modern and impressive groups of educational buildings with separate quarters for the various courses in the curriculum. Even the roads have taken on the appearance of permanent thoroughfares, broken occasionally by bridges of architectual beauty and design. A magnificent system of national and local parks has been set aside for the enjoyment and recreation of those who have time to travel. Vehicles have been built and equipped in a fashion that allows the traveler every comfort and convenience. Places of amusement have been arranged so as to appeal to the artistic taste and emotion of the people of leisure. Powerful machinery has taken the place of hundreds of thousands of workmen who formerly served under circumstances detrimental to their physical and mental well-being. These people have been released for positions more in keeping with the ordinary taste and culture of normal individuals. All of these give evidence of the substantial material progress and social interest of the people whose labor made such expansion possible.

Between the lower limit of the realm of necessity and the upper limit of the realm of luxury most of our people live. In times of extreme prosperity many push forward into the realm of luxury, while in times of depression great numbers fall back into the realm of necessity. This is not a classification of our people but of circumstances under which they live. We move freely from one state of affairs to another. Many of us rise and fall with the economic tide. Personal freedom provides for this possibility. Our American sense of fair play has helped us to believe that everyone should have the right and the privilege to live in the realm of luxury, that is, if our judgment and ability allows such attainment. However, this luxury must not consist of the things that we possess but in what we do and achieve for others by means of these things. We must remember that with some there is luxury in simplicity while with others there is poverty in the midst of much.

DEMOCRATIC ASSISTANCE AND CONTROL

All agree that we have a right to experience the best in life, but we must limit, if we can, the conditions under which men live. Not a single citizen of our great country in the midst of plenty should be permitted to live below the realm of necessity. At this point the group as a whole must assist the individual. On the other hand, no one should either desire or be protected in the privilege of living above the realm of luxury. Here again the group must take an interest in the direction and control of the individual. The former for the most part live in the realm of poverty while the latter indulge in extravagance. People deprived of the ordinary necessities of life on the one extreme and those smothered with extraordinary possessions on the other, both present social and economic problems of an acute nature. Poverty breeds disease, crime, and discontent, while extravagance nurtures the germs of idleness, selfishness, and immorality. They both create an atmosphere of pessimism and depression. How to assist the former and control the latter without destroying their initiative and at the same time furnish guidance for the great central group is a governmental concern of the first magnitude.

If the lack of interest and initiative force a certain per cent of the first group into the pit of poverty, no government, no matter how strong, can lift them out. Government cannot enter the domain of individual personality and arouse there that which has not responded to the kindly efforts of the home, the school, and the church. It can and docs, however, provide public institutions wherein these people may enjoy the necessities of life. But along with the maladjusted people already mentioned they lose their liberty. The remainder of this group must be helped, but in order not to destroy their initiative either by letting them receive directly from the government provisions for which they give nothing in return, or by compelling them to compete with the government in the field of private enterprise, such help should be considered from the standpoint of extra-constitutional assistance. This problem is always acute in periods of depression. To such calls as this our people have always responded, and by so doing we have kept alive that fine spirit of voluntary social helpfulness.

To control those who would live in extravagance and use any means, just or unjust, to enjoy this privilege, presents an issue of great consequence. It is always acute in times of prosperity. While changing customs which affect prices and periods of depression at times serve as restraining agencies, nevertheless the government must act. Its control must be direct and definite. Our government has assumed this responsibility.

Now the necessity of controlling these two groups of citizens has a tendency to distort our vision of the real function of government as applied to the problem of the great majority of our citizens who enjoy the privilege of moving about in the realms of necessity, convenience, and luxury because of the chances involved. This chance-taking attitude of our people stimulates initiative and this in turn makes possible wholesome competition.

We expect the government, which we ourselves sanction or make, to guide and regulate our collective activity, but we would not have it curtail our ordered liberty. We retain the right to exercise individual judgment even though we face competition which creates an economic state of affairs not altogether simple from the standpoint of government. Perhaps some day we shall learn to compete with our own economic record rather than with that of another.

Paradoxical as it may seem, competition in any line of industrial or of commercial activity when carried to the extreme, leads to the destruction of the social order, while cooperation in any line of human endeavor when carried to the extreme, usually results in a combine which destroys individual initiative and effort. In the first instance the individual assumes autocratic authority, while in the second the group assumes this power. The problem is not so much whether the individual or the group becomes responsible at any particular period where the shortcomings of society are involved, but whether or not the individual or the group uses methods which make for democratic enterprise. Of course it must readily be admitted that the nature of the case would resolve the decision in favor of the group. This is because there is opportunity for the use of checks and balances at times when choices or decisions have to be made. Then too, there is greater likelihood of compromise where more than one individual assumes authority for the action of the group. In thinking of this problem as a national issue the government takes the place of the group in the smaller community or locality. It is probably true that the most difficult if not dangerous problem arises in times when the government is confronted with industrial organization on a large scale. President Hoover takes account of this situation in the following words:

"The entrance of the Government began strongly three decades ago, when our industrial organization began to move powerfully in the direction of consolidation of enterprise. We found in the course of this development that equality of opportunity and its corollary, individual initiative, was being throttled by the concentration of control of industry and service, and thus an economic domination of groups builded over the nation. At this time, particularly, we were threatened with a form of autocracy of economic power. Our mass of regulation of public utilities and our legislation against restraint of trade is the monument to our intent to preserve an equality of opportunity. This regulation is itself proof that we have gone a long way toward the abandonment of the 'capitalism of Adam Smith.'"

A real solution to the problem of guidance and regulation is found when self-interest is tempered with a sense of human service. Self-interest alone seeks individual progress and security with the help but not the sanction of the group, while self-interest blended with the thought of public service wants exactly the same results with both the approval and assistance of the group. Success attained with the consent and through the guidance of the group brings progress, prosperity, and security to all, and thereby safeguards these to the individual. In such an environment self-regardfulness supplants selfish interest. Mr. Hoover sees the validity of this idea and comments thus:

"Today business organization is moving strongly

toward cooperation. There are in the cooperative great hopes that we can even gain in individuality, equality of opportunity, and an enlarged field for initiative, and at the same time reduce many of the great wastes of over-reckless competition in production and distribution. Those who either congratulate themselves or those who fear that cooperation is an advance toward socialism need neither rejoice nor worry. Cooperation in its current economic sense represents the initiative of self-interest blended with a sense of service, for nobody belongs to a cooperative who is not striving to sell his products or services for more or striving to buy from others for less or striving to make his income more secure. Their members are furnishing the capital for extension of their activities just as effectively as if they did it in corporate form and they are simply transferring the profit principle from joint return to individual return. Their only success lies where they eliminate waste either in production or distribution—and they can do neither if they destroy individual initiative. Indeed, this phase of development of our individualism promises to become the dominant note of its 20th Century expansion. But it will thrive only in so far as it can construct leadership and a sense of service, and so long as it preserves the initiative and safeguards the individuality of its members."

Either competition or cooperation, when entered into with a distinct feeling of authority on the part of the employers or directors and a feeling of obedience on the part of the worker or workers leads to but one result, namely, drudgery. For whenever an individual enters any occupation, task, or activity with divided attention, drudgery ensues. Work without interest is much the same as taxation without representation. The psychological or spiritual aspect of the effort is lacking. But let us examine the positive phase of this problem. Either competition or cooperation, when entered into with a distinct feeling of service on the part of the employers or directors and a feeling of shared experience on the part of the worker or workers leads to but one result—the development of a spirit of mutual helpfulness. Personal satisfaction is the outcome. The problem in this field is not so much one of changing a system as one of creating a satisfactory motive, for in the long run motives have more power over systems than systems have over motives.

In view of these facts, then, what shall we say concerning our American ideal of individual liberty in industrial and commercial organizations?

Perhaps there are many leaders who would answer—profit. And no student of economics can deny that the compelling urge of financial gain has influenced the method of control of many business concerns. But if the American government accepts this goal as the ideal toward which we shall move, then the principle of individual liberty in the field of economics will no longer be effective. Our civilization will turn in the wrong direction. Let us ask Mr. Hoover to express an opinion on this important phase of our economic system. If we ask him a question concerning the selfish motive of business he will respond by asking another: "Do not our merchants and business men pride themselves in something of service given beyond the price of their goods?"

No man in public life has answered this question with more clarity, emphasis, and conviction than has the thirty-first president of our republic. If we understand him correctly, and we believe we do, in all industry and business, among all employers and employees, he would supplant the emotion of fear with the emotion of confidence, the virtue of extreme prudence with the virtue of adventure, and the ambition of profit or gain with the ambition of service. To him the idea of service carries a challenge of adventure. It takes place in an atmosphere of confidence rather than fear. Its stimulus is a desire to be helpful. Nowhere in his program of service is the concept of servitude admitted.

The modern manufacturer who believes in the high ideals of American individualism as outlined by Mr. Hoover is not a slave serving a community of people. He, as an industrial leader, is free within the limits of his own trade. He serves the public through the products he manufactures, but at the same time he is the servant of his associates and employees. He appreciates the validity of the principle that, "If any man would be first, he shall be last of all, and servant of all."

This dual service ideal is making rapid progress

here in America due to the beneficent influence of the service clubs of our cities. A new code of business and industrial ethics making service its pivotal point is evolving. In this code provision is made for the free expression of individuality without interfering with that recently developed method of work called shared experience. As these standards evolve the philosophic theory of individuation and the political doctrine of collectivism fuse into the principle of American individualism which, as we have learned, is cooperative rather than competitive.

But if we admit, and admit we must, that the ideal of service is by no means universal in business, how shall we prevent the industrial leader, or leaders, whose vision of mutual helpfulness is clouded, from exploiting the individual worker and disregarding the interests of the people?

In answering this question we must not overemphasize the negative aspect of government, since "Government," says Mr. Hoover, "is only in part a negative function. Its purpose is not merely to stand as a watchman over what is forbidden: government must be a constructive force."

At least one of the primary functions of democratic government is to keep open the stream of progress, sometimes by dredging the channel and sometimes by erecting dams. The former method is synonymous with stimulation, the latter with the organization of controls. But it must always be remembered that both methods deepen the stream. Some in our country would largely confine governmental activity to the work of dredging while others equally conscientious would direct a large amount of energy to the task of dam building. As a constructive force the government assumes the responsibility of encouraging a proper attitude toward industry and of regulating by law certain business practices inimical to the good of the worker and the public. President Hoover has a clear and definite proposal in this connection:

"In recent years we have established a differentiation in the whole method of business regulation between the industries which produce and distribute commodities on the one hand and public utilities on the other. In the former, our laws insist upon effective competition; in the latter, because we substantially confer a monopoly by limiting competition, we must regulate their services and rates. The rigid enforcement of the laws applicable to both groups is the very base of equal opportunity and freedom from domination for all our people, and it is just as essential for the stability and prosperity of business itself as for the protection of the public at large. Such regulation should be extended by the Federal Government within the limitations of the Constitution and only when the individual States are without power to protect their citizens through their own authority. On the other hand, we should be fearless when the authority rests only in the Federal Government."

In this connection attention should be called to one negative phase of government with which President Hoover is vitally concerned. No public official has attacked the problem with more courage and zeal than he. That the government must not go into business is with him a conviction of compelling significance.

"I insist," says he, "upon the most strict regulation of public utilities, because otherwise they would destroy equality of opportunity. I object to the government going into business in competition with its citizens because that would destroy equality of opportunity. And equality of opportunity is the flux with which alone we can melt out full and able leadership to the nation."

Again he says:

"Bureaucracy is ever desirous of spreading its influence and its power. You cannot extend the mastery of the government over the daily working life of a people without at the same time making it the master of the people's souls and thoughts. Every expansion of government in business means that government in order to protect itself from the political consequences of its errors and wrongs is driven irresistibly without peace to greater and greater control of the nation's press and platform. Free speech does not live many hours after free industry and free commerce die. . . . Liberalism is a force truly of the spirit, a force proceeding from the deep realization that economic freedom cannot be sacrificed if political freedom is to be preserved. Even if governmental conduct of business could give us more efficiency instead of less efficiency, the fundamental

objection to it would remain unaltered and un-
abated. It would destroy political equality. It would
increase rather than decrease abuse and corruption.
It would stifle initiative and invention. It would
undermine the development of leadership. It would
cramp and cripple the mental and spiritual energies
of our people. It would extinguish equality and opportunity. It would dry up the spirit of liberty and
progress. For these reasons primarily it must be
resisted. For a hundred and fifty years liberalism
has found its true spirit in the American system, not
in the European systems."

Another statement will serve to show that Mr.
Hoover believes that the ideal of service is being
built into our industrial system and that more and
more it will become effective because it deals with
the foundation motives of business.

"Indeed, there are deep and promising currents
originating in our economic life driving toward a
mutualization of public and private interests, em-
ployer and employee interest with promise of a new
period in industrial development. There has been
a genuine growth of business conscience and service,
and this growth is far more precious than any
amount of legislation."

ECONOMIC FREEDOM

At this point, inasmuch as we are concerned with
the problem of individualism in business, it is only
fair to ask, by what standard shall we measure the
liberty of the workman? Or shall we grant him the

right to be economically free? Mr. Hoover responds with an answer that almost startles even the most liberal social philosopher or progressive political economist:

"Equality of opportunity is the right of every American—rich or poor, foreign or native-born, irrespective of faith or color. It is the right of every individual to attain that position in life to which his ability and character entitle him. By its maintenance we will alone hold open the door of opportunity to every new generation, to every boy and girl. It tolerates no privileged classes or castes or groups who would hold opportunity as their prerogative. Only from confidence that this right will be upheld can flow that unbounded courage and hope which stimulate each individual man and woman to endeavor and to achievement. The sum of their achievement is the gigantic harvest of national progress."

As we read such words we sometimes feel that the author is stating a general economic principle without actually taking into consideration human need. But if anyone doubts the sincerity of the interest Mr. Hoover has in the workman regardless of the field in which he is engaged, he need but to consider a further statement, in which he challenges economic leaders with a new industrial philosophy. His words carry the cordial endorsement of men whose vision of the needs of others is expressed in a most advanced system of moral precepts:

"Moreover, the purpose of industry is only in

part to create objects, articles, and services which satisfy physical needs. This is an essential function; but the higher purpose of industry is to provide satisfactions of life to human beings not alone in its products but in the work of production itself. Unless industry makes living men and women and children happier in their work, unless it gives opportunity and creative satisfactions in the job itself, it can not excuse its failure by pleading that at least it has kept them alive. Man learned the art of staying alive long before he learned the art of mechanics. The machine must build him a better life, not alone in time of leisure but in joy of work, than he knew before. I have every faith that in the broad view it is doing so, not only in its products and relief from sweat, but that it increasingly enlarges man's satisfactions in his toil. And year by year do we realize more of our responsibilities in the human relations within industry. Mechanization is so distinctive of our modern civilization that even as a mechanical conception we often tend to forget that the most wonderful and powerful machine in the world is the men and women themselves. It is the human being from which achievement is won far more than the tool.

"However astonishing may be the increase in usefulness of machines as they grow in size and ingenuity, their improvement is little as compared with the enlarged effectiveness of organized intelligence and cooperation when men pool their efforts to achieve a common end. Man's conquest of machines is less spectacular than his conquest of his own will."

In the same address from which the preceding paragraphs were taken, President Hoover commended the men who served a great industry in the following words:

"To build up and preserve unbroken a cooperative spirit between a great group of employers and employees for two long generations is a cheering proof of the possibilities of human nature. The secret of it is more important to mankind than any secret of trade, or any new invention.

"Fortunately there is nothing mysterious about it, nothing patentable or exclusive, nothing that is not free to be used by all. The key to it is as old as the religions we profess. Its origins and its power lie in generations of education and scientific research, in the benignant forces of mutual good-will, the spirit of mutual helpfulness, the virtues of patience and toleration and understanding."

No one can read these words, if he credits Mr. Hoover with intellectual honesty, without knowing that he considers human rights above property rights. To foster "creative satisfaction" in the worker is an objective worthy of the efforts of the most successful men of affairs. It puts the individual and his family above ambition for financial profit. Mr. Hoover, as every one else, realizes that "this experience may not be universal. If it were, the world would be wealthier in spirit by incalculable enrichments of human happiness."

"He would be a rash man who would state that we can produce the economic millennium, but there is great assurance that America is finding herself upon the road to secure social satisfaction, with the preservation of private industry, initiative, and full opportunity for the development of the individual.

"It is true that these economic things are not the objective of life itself. If by their steady improvement we shall yet farther reduce poverty, shall create and secure more happy homes, we shall have served to make better men and women and a greater Nation."

Now if our government can encourage the motive of service, and we believe it can, in our business and industrial leaders and at the same time give assistance to or assume control of marginal groups or individuals, either below the realm of necessity or beyond the limits of luxury while allowing freedom to those capable of self-direction, and by so doing help give direction to our social and industrial systems so as to let the workman find creative satisfaction in his vocation, trade, or profession, we shall have made some progress in the field of political economy. This, we as a nation are trying to do. We ask for the government and for our people as a national group only that which we asked for the individual—the right to set up an aim and the privilege of outlining plans of action that will make the aim a reality.

President Hoover, as a national leader, has proposed an aim worthy of the devotion of every citizen of this great republic because it gives direction to our conscious effort.

"Our purpose," says he, "is to build in this nation a human society, not an economic system. We wish to increase the efficiency and productivity of our country, but its final purpose is happier homes. We shall succeed through the faith, the loyalty, the self-sacrifice, the devotion to eternal ideals which live today in every American."

But we must always remember that while our aim remains constant, our methods may change because we are a growing people. President Hoover does not overlook this item as he tries to draw a mental picture of our economic system:

"Many vital changes and movements of vast proportions are taking place in the economic world. The effect of these changes upon the future cannot be seen clearly as yet. Of this, however, we are sure: Our system, based upon the ideals of individual initiative and of equality of opportunity, is not an artificial thing. Rather, it is the outgrowth of the experience of America, and expresses the faith and spirit of our people. It has carried us in a century and a half to leadership of the economic world. If our economic system does not match our highest expectations at all times, it does not require revolutionary action to bring it into accord with any necessity that experience may prove. It has successfully adjusted itself to changing conditions in the past. It will do so again. The mobility of our institutions, the richness of our resources, and the abilities of our people enable us to meet them unafraid."

If under the urge of ordered freedom the individual enjoyed "creative action" he should under the compelling power of these governmental and economic ideals find "creative satisfaction." Mr. Hoover's principles of American Individualism in the field of economics demand just this. He has found a new political theory for a new day, for, says he, "governments are tested at last by their attitudes to the welfare of men and women."

POPULAR RESPONSIBILITY

But the people must be willing to assume some responsibility. At least we must cooperate in maintaining our political freedom in connection with our economic expansion.

In the autumn of 1929 Mr. Edward G. Lowry called the attention of the readers of the Century Magazine to a state of affairs in our country which as we look back upon it now, held the possibility of governmental disaster. His description of our mental condition, without being too critical, pictured the possibility of a drift toward a reactionary program. Said he,

"President Hoover faces an interesting and a changing world—faces it composedly, eagerly, unafraid. By our choice Mr. Hoover is in temporary command of the ship upon which we are passengers; we are relying on him to know and to indicate from time to time the direction and rate of our progress, although we are apparently more concerned about being comfortable on the trip than we are about our destination."

Mr. Hoover's unselfish governmental ideal blocked the tragedy that might have happened late that year, for whenever a people for any reason whether logical or illogical, loses its sense of direction without developing a feeling of distress, its government is in danger of exploitation. Whenever we become more concerned about being comfortable than we are about our destination, the way is open for leaders to assume the power of a dictator. This is particularly true when we face an economic depression. From every hamlet, village, city, and state of our great nation there came a demand for a leader of authority. People turned to the federal government for the solution of their private community problems. They demanded action of a type inconsistent with the foundation principles of our republic. They made governmental demands upon the President to which he could not respond without assuming the rôle of an autocrat which he deliberately and consistently refused to do. Accordingly, it would be hard to imagine a situation more favorable to the development of a strong centralized autocratic form of government than during the present presidential term of office. Many people have been willing to let the government do for them that which no democratic government should ever do. We asked him as a public official to enter private enterprise. Mr.

Hoover knew that in the long run we would not want that which we demanded because it would be contrary to our best interests.

When he assumed leadership in the hour of crisis his program included, first of all, the preservation of the fundamental principles upon which our American way of life depended. His decision was based upon experience, the roots of which penetrated into the past of many historic civilizations. He chose the slow and difficult way of placing the responsibility for the action of our nation squarely upon the shoulders of local leaders and representatives where it rightly belongs. By so doing he was protecting the inalienable right of every individual citizen of America by refusing to be moved by the compelling challenges of a temporary crisis. When he could have become the world's greatest dictator, he chose to remain the servant of his people.

In one of his campaign addresses he said, "The Presidency is no dictatorship. It is not intended to be. Safeguards are provided to prevent it. Our fathers knew that men were not made for government but government for men—to aid and to serve them. Our government rests solely upon the will of the people; it springs from the people; its policies must be approved by the people."

More than two years after he became President he said:

"For the first time in history the Federal Government has taken an extensive and positive part in mitigating the effects of depression and expediting

recovery. I have conceived that if we would preserve our democracy this leadership must take the
part not of attempted dictatorship but of organizing
cooperation in the constructive forces of the community and of stimulating every element of initiative
and self-reliance in the country. There is no sudden
stroke of either governmental or private action
which can dissolve these world difficulties; patient,
constructive action in a multitude of directions is the
strategy of success. This battle is upon a thousand
fronts.

"We have assured the country from panic and its
hurricane of bankruptcy by coordinated action between the Treasury, the Federal reserve system, the
banks, the Farm Loan and Farm Board system. We
have steadily urged the maintenance of wages and
salaries, preserving American standards of living,
not alone for its contribution to consumption of
goods but with the far greater purpose of maintaining social good-will through avoiding industrial conflict with its sufferng and social disorder. We are
maintaining organized cooperation with industry systematically to distribute the available work, so as to
give income to as many families as possible. We
have reversed the traditional policy in depressions of
reducing expenditures upon construction work. We
are maintaining a steady expansion of ultimately
needed construction work in cooperation with the
States, municipalities, and industries. Over two bil-
lions of dollars is being expended, and to-day a
million men are being given direct and indirect em-

ployment through these enlarged activities. We have sustained the people in 21 States who faced dire disaster from the drought. We are giving aid and support to the farmers in marketing their crops, by which they have realized hundreds of millions more in prices than the farmers of any other country. Through the tariff we are saving our farmers and workmen from being overwhelmed with goods from foreign countries where, even since our tariff was revised, wages and prices have been reduced to much lower levels than before. We are holding down taxation by exclusion of every possible governmental expenditure not absolutely essential or needed in increase of employment or assistance to the farmers. We are rigidly excluding immigration until our own people are employed. The departures and deportations to-day actually exceed arrivals. We are maintaining and will maintain systematic voluntary organization in the community in aid of employment and care for distress. There are a score of other directions in which cooperation is organized and stimulation is given."

After enumerating all these activities, with all the courage his high office requires, he said:

"We propose to go forward with these major activities and policies. We will not be diverted from them. By these and other measures which shall develop as the occasion shall require, we shall keep this ship steady in the storm."

Mr. Hoover's record as an executive before his election to the presidency had popularized him to a degree that would have made it easy for him to have declared the existence of an emergency which would naturally have demanded autocratic leadership. He could easily have used the methods made popular by the recent war, to which people everywhere pointed with the pride of a victorious nation, but his administration assumed the task of replacing the methods used for war promotion with the methods of constructive, orderly, cooperative effort. To this work he set his head and his hand with a devotion that will be recognized by students interested in the preservation of American Individualism and in the success of democratic government as an achievement unparalleled in this period of political confusion.

In times of extreme national difficulty clear vision and sound judgment are two executive qualities which thinking people demand of their statesmen.

But there are periods when the executive must have more than these. He must not only see clearly the issues involved in a given complex situation, such as an economic depression world-wide in scope, and use good judgment in making a series of decisions, but he must understand its causes as well, some of which may not be apparent to the lay mind either because of prejudice or lack of evidence. Confronted with such a state of affairs, the real statesman must determine the cause of a condition, and then have courage to propose the remedy even though it may arouse antagonistic reactions among the people whom he tries to help. Such action demands courage of the highest order—courage born of unselfish determination to serve. Successful democracy demands that the people shall have an equal courage in order to follow their leader.

We must now turn our thought to a discussion of the institution of war, which because of its inherent nature is diametrically opposed to that which has been said about our American way of life.

CHAPTER V

American Individualism and the Problem of War

A Dual Problem. The President's Point of View. Aggressive Good-will. Public Opinion and Concentrated Effort. Cooperative Individualism.

"War is destruction, and we should blame war for its injustices, not a social system whose object is construction. The submergence of the individual, however, in the struggle of the race could be but temporary—its continuance through the crushing of individual action and its inequities would, if for no other reason, destroy the foundations of our civilization."

H. H.

CHAPTER V

American Individualism and the Problem of War

A DUAL PROBLEM

PRESIDENT HOOVER is deeply conscious of the fact that either the destructive methods of war must be supplanted by constructive methods of reason, or our ideal of American Individualism must be abandoned. He is familiar with the historical development of two antagonistic philosophies which have grown side by side in our national life over a period of approximately three centuries. Sufficient evidence is at hand to show that we inherited war as a ready-made instrument of control or defense, while we have developed the principle of American Individualism through experience and reason. As he deals with these opposite points of view the President assumes the attitude of a patient and painstaking councilor and conciliator. Because of the remarkable achievement attained by our government in every phase of life he cannot surrender that for which the people of this country have so diligently labored since the beginning of our nation. He must preserve that quality of individual personality which the government was organized to assist. He must not deal lightly with the individual convictions of his fellow countrymen nor permit even a temporary suspension of his abiding faith in the American way of life and system of government.

With these facts before us, what shall we say of his attitude of mind and methods of procedure as he confronts the greatest obstacle to the further development of our individualistic manner of life?

As one reviews with President Hoover in his executive office at the White House some of the national and international questions before the world today he is impressed with the dual aspect of practically every problem. The visitor quickly understands that he is conferring with a man whose human interest and kindly sympathy embrace the welfare of the individual citizens of America and the world. He finds him anxious to consider every problem from the human point of view. And yet he sees lying on the desk before him official documents which represent organizations, institutions, and governments which cannot easily and quickly adjust themselves to new demands.

He is at once in a proper attitude to ask the President how he is able to correlate his fundamental principles of peace with his duties as Commander-in-chief of the American Army and Navy. He does not have to wait for a reply. The President immediately responds by calling attention to the fact that we are living in two worlds—the real and the ideal. Until we reach the ideal state of civilization we must deal with the customs and conventions as they are, while at the same time we must make every effort to create a more satisfactory condition. He has upon numerous occasions stated his views in language so clear and forceful that we can no longer question his position.

THE PRESIDENT'S POINT OF VIEW

His aversion to war grew out of a friendly philosophy of life learned in youth which he later tested by all the tragedies of war itself. He says that "Those who really know war never glorify it. I have seen too much of the tragic sufferings of men, women, and children, of the black shadows that ever run on the heels of war, to wish to recall those scenes. I hope never to see them again."

Few men have been able to visualize more clearly for the people of his country the human aspect of war. In his inaugural address he individualizes the problem and compels personal consideration of it:

"It is impossible, my countrymen, to speak of peace without profound emotion. In thousands of homes in America, in millions of homes around the world, there are vacant chairs. It would be a shameful confession of our unworthiness if it should develop that we have abandoned the hope for which all these men died. Surely civilization is old enough, surely mankind is mature enough so that we ought in our lifetime to find a way to permanent peace."

Because of his broad and comprehensive international outlook and his intense interest in creating a better world situation he has dared to attempt to find a way to permanent peace. In his Armistice Day Address in 1931 he outlined a course of action that appears reasonable and logical when considered in view of the present world situation. He recognized the demand of a practical political order while at the same time he gave consideration to the inspiring challenge of the ideal world.

"However great our desire for peace, we must not assume that the peace for which these men died has become assured to the world or that the obligations which they left to us, the living, have been discharged. The minds of many races still are stirred by memories of centuries of injustice; in others there is ever present the fear of invasion and domination; many peoples are filled with hopes of liberty and independence. The boundaries of many nations are but zones of age-old contention. The growth of population and economic striving press against the borders of others.

"World-wide expansion of commerce and industry, with its vast interchange of citizens, brings the daily obligation of self-respecting nations to see that their nationals abroad in pacific pursuits shall not be unjustly imperiled as to life and property. In every country men can secure public attention and even a living by stirring malignant forces of fear and hate of their neighbors. As a result of these forces the world is more heavily armed than even before the great war.

"All of these dangers present to statesmen a world where peace cannot be had by resolution and injunction alone. Peace is the product of preparedness for defense, of the patient settlement of controversy, and the dynamic development of the forces of good will. It is the result of the delicate balance of that realism born of human experience and of idealism born of the highest of human aspirations for international justice."

His plan for the promotion of peace clearly involves a program of national defense and the creation of a spirit of world-wide good will. His attitude toward the first suggestion should be made perfectly clear before we discuss the second proposal. We cannot misinterpret his point of view when we read the following words:

"Certainly until the peace machinery of the world has been developed and tested over long years we must maintain such forces of defense as will at every moment prevent the penetration of a hostile force over our borders. And our security to-day is well assured by an Army and Navy whose high tradition of valor and skill is represented in both the command and ranks of to-day and we shall maintain it."

Without question President Hoover believes in the maintenance of an armed force adequate for national defense. But as President of this great country he cannot limit his interest to this phase of the question, because he does "not measure the future of America in terms of our lifetime."

"Our problem," says he, "is to assure the adjustment of our forces to the minimum based upon the outlook in the world; to strive for lower armament throughout the whole world; to promote good will among nations; to conduct our military activities with rigid economy; to prevent extremists on one side from undermining the public will to support our necessary forces, and to prevent extremists on the other side from waste of public funds."

As he considers the needs of America in its relationship with other nations, he finds an annual world expenditure on all arms of nearly $5,000,000,000 which is an increase of approximately seventy per cent over the yearly cost before the war. He does not overlook the fact that nearly 5,500,000 men are actively under arms with 20,000,000 more in reserve. While he is "not unaware of the difficulties of this question" he is certain that the stability of the world requires fearless action in the matter of arms reduction. "This vast armament continues not only a burden upon the economic recuperation of the world, but, of even more consequence, the constant threats and fears which arise from it are a serious contribution to all forms of instability, whether social, political, or economic. Endeavor as we must in support of every proposal of international economic cooperation that is just to our respective peoples, yet we must recognize that reduction of this gigantic waste of competition in military establishments is in the ultimate of an importance transcendent over all other forms of such economic effort."

AGGRESSIVE GOOD-WILL

If now we keep in mind these considerations which make clear his attitude toward national defense and world reduction of arms we shall be able to appreciate his second proposal which involves a program of aggressive good will. He emphatically declares that "International confidence cannot be builded upon fear—it must be builded upon good will. The whole history of the world is filled with chapters of the failure to secure peace through either competitive arms or intimidation."

No one is more certain than he that if the irresistible power of good will is to supplant the force of arms, international controversies must be settled through the patient negotiation of difficulties by national representatives who derive their authority from world inclusive treaties and agreements supported by an intelligent public opinion.

When the history of the twentieth century is written, if it is written accurately and without political bias, it will carry the story covering the incident of the proclamation of the Peace Pact by President Herbert Hoover. It will say that when the president laid down his pen after affixing his signature to that document, that the greatest agreement ever conceived in the thought of man and subscribed to by the people of America through their official representatives became effective.

Mr. Hoover had been elected by a group of American citizens whose representatives assembled in convention in the summer of 1928 declared that:

"We endorse the proposal of the Secretary of State for a multilateral treaty proposed to the principal powers of the world, to be open to the signatures of all nations, to renounce war as an instrument of national policy and declaring in favor of pacific settlement of international disputes, the first step in outlawing war. The idea has stirred the conscience of mankind and gained widespread approval, both of Governments and of people, and the conclusion of the treaty will be acclaimed as the greatest single step in history toward the conservation of peace."

Having been elected upon such a platform his satisfaction in signing the Peace Pact proclamation must have been three-fold. He was keeping faith with his supporters; he was the leader of a movement that was cordially supported by both political parties; and he was acting as the personal representative of millions of peace minded people the world over. The Pact was in a broad and comprehensive sense a nonpartisan document. It carried the approval of men and women in all walks of American life.

Early in the afternoon of July 24, 1929, the day upon which President Hoover proclaimed The General Pact for the Renunciation of War, he made the following statement which shows as effectively as a printed message can, the significance of his act:

"That (The Peace Pact) was a proposal to the conscience and idealism of civilized nations. It suggested a new step in international law, rich with meaning, pregnant with new ideas in the conduct of world relations. It represented a platform from which there is instant appeal to the public opinion of the world as to specific acts and deeds. . . . I congratulate this assembly, the states it represents, and indeed, the entire world upon the coming into force of this additional instrument of humane endeavor to do away with war as an instrument of national policy and to obtain by pacific means alone the settlement of international disputes.

"I am glad of this opportunity to pay merited tribute to the two statesmen whose names the world has properly adopted in its designation of this Treaty. To Aristide Briand, Minister of Foreign Affairs of France, we owe the inception of the Treaty and to his zeal is due a very large share of the success which attended the subsequent negotiations. To Frank B. Kellogg, then Secretary of State of the United States, we owe its expansion to the proportions of a treaty open to the entire world and destined, as I most confidently hope, shortly to include among its parties every country of the world.

"Mr. Stimson has sent forward today a message of felicitation to Mr. Briand and to the people of France for whom he speaks. I am happy, Mr. Kellogg, to extend to you, who represented the people of the United States with such untiring devotion and with such a high degree of diplomatic skill in the negotiations of this treaty, their everlasting gratitude.

"We are honored here by the presence of President Coolidge under whose administration this great step in world peace was initiated. Under his authority and with his courageous support you, Mr. Kellogg, succeeded in this great service. And I wish to mark also the high appreciation in which we hold

Senators Borah and Swanson for their leadership during its confirmation in the Senate.

"May I ask you who represent Governments which have accepted this Treaty, now a part of their supreme law and their most sacred obligations, to convey to them the high appreciation of the Government of the United States that through their cordial collaboration an act so auspicious for the future happiness of mankind has now been consummated? I dare predict that the influence of the Treaty for the Renunciation of War will be felt in a large proportion of all future international acts. The magnificent opportunity and the compelling duty now open to us should spur us on to the fulfillment of every opportunity that is calculated to implement this treaty and to extend the policy which it so nobly sets forth."

The pact which he proclaimed carried a short but world inclusive agreement. It was simple, direct and clear. It was not a statement that had within its words a magic power capable of preventing all future international misunderstandings but it was an agreement that furnished the foundation of a new world order. It was crowded into two short paragraphs:

"Article I.—The High Contracting Parties solemnly declare, in the names of their respective peoples, that they condemn recourse to war for the solution of international controversies, and renounce it as an instrument of national policy in their relations with one another.

"Article II.—The High Contracting Parties agree

that the settlement or solution of all disputes or conflicts, of whatever nature or of whatever origin they may be, which may arise among them, shall never be sought except by pacific means. . . ."

Its intent could not be questioned. It meant to make possible a warless world. It delegalized an institution with a background covering many thousands of years. It was a daring and courageous action which our President and Senate took. But the Chief Executive had prepared his associates, the people of the United States for such action by declaring in his inaugural address that: "The United States fully accepts the profound truth that our own progress, prosperity and peace are interlocked with the progress, prosperity, and peace of all humanity."

The legislative and executive action necessary to make the agreement binding was of course not an isolated incident in government affairs. For more than a decade public opinion had been crystallizing in favor of methods and legal procedure that would make future war impossible. A new world interest had taken form. Everywhere ministers, educators, and statesmen were discussing world peace.

In America, this interest, aside from being inherent in the situation, that is, a natural reaction to the tragedy of war, was stimulated or aroused by the many utterances of President Woodrow Wilson. In 1919 he stood in France overlooking the graves of the soldiers whom he, as Commander-in-Chief of the Army and Navy, had sent to the battle front. In such a situation he felt the compulsion of the spirit of service in which those men had given their lives. With all the power of his personality he challenged the thoughts of his contemporaries when he said— "It is our duty to take and maintain the safeguards which will see to it that the mothers of America and the mothers of France and England and Italy and Belgium and all other suffering nations should never be called upon for this sacrifice again. This can be done. It must be done. And it will be done."

Just ten years to the day after President Wilson had uttered this prophecy, President Hoover said of this document that was intended to make his prediction come true:

"That is a declaration that springs from the aspirations and hearts of men and women throughout the world. It is a solemn covenant to which the great nations of the world have bound themselves. . . . But, if this agreement is to fulfill its high purpose we and other nations must accept its consequences; we must clothe faith and idealism with action. That action must march with the inexorable tread of common sense and realism to accomplishment. . . . It implies that nations will conduct their daily intercourse in keeping with the spirit of that agreement. It implies that we shall endeavor to develop those instrumentalities of peaceful adjustment that will enable us to remove disputes from the field of emotion to the field of calm and judicial consideration."

President Wilson was anxious that the United States keep the promise he as chief executive had made to the men who were subject to the draft, namely, that we were fighting a war to end war. President Hoover recognized this obligation at the end of the decade when he said:

"A solemn obligation lies upon us to press forward in our pursuit of those things for which they died. Our duty is to seek ever new and widening opportunities to insure the world against the horror and irretrievable wastage of war. Much has been done, but we must wage peace continuously, with the same energy as they waged war."

It is an obligation that neither he nor any other public or private citizen can face without solemn thought and resolve. He could say later that, "We were sincere when we signed that pact. We engaged our national honor when we ratified it."

This we believe is the attitude of the people of our Republic.

Now international treaty making involves problems similar to those confronted by the builders of our national government during the early days of our republic. In a word, the one was a question of understanding, the other a problem of control. The former required interaction through representation, the latter demanded organization by means of legal procedure. Such governmental demands inspired public men to plead for the development of a national rather than a sectional interest. A little over one hundred years ago on the seventeenth of June, in an address at the laying of the cornerstone of Bunker Hill monument, Daniel Webster pleaded:

"Let our object be, our country, our whole country, and nothing but our country." To this call our people responded and we have built here a mighty nation. Our mechanical means of communication came at just the right time to make possible a national consciousness. Without these instruments our tendency to be sectionally minded might have separated our country into distinct units in spite of our representative government and our legal agreements.

Let us consider, for purposes of inspiration and encouragement, some of the devices that make possible communication which in the final analysis is the basis of mutual understanding, local, national, and international. It appears to be an axiomatic fact that if we have good-will toward people we must have some means of knowing them.

To evaluate the contribution of the American Railway System as a common carrier of goods and people is a task far too extensive for our purpose here. However, a cursory survey of its yearly service readily suggests its value as a medium of human contact. The officers have control of more than four hundred and twenty-five thousand miles of track, while the employees drive more than sixty thousand locomotives. They carry approximately eight hundred million passengers and one billion, three hundred and seventy million revenue tons of freight. The interaction of people and the exchange of thought through the exchange of commodities, made possible by this means of travel and communication alone, would be sufficient to hold the American people together in a bond of national idealism.

The owners of the twenty-two million automobiles registered last year have for their use, and maintained at public expense, more than three million miles of roads outside of the limits of our cities. Inasmuch as fourteen billion gallons of gas are used, the automobile drivers cover a distance annually, at a conservative estimate, of one hundred and sixty-eight billion miles. Social contacts made through this means of travel give opportunity to understand the customs and traditions of other people and thereby create a spirit of good-will.

The past quarter of a century has given us another means of contact—the airplane. Forty aircraft companies now have routes covering approximately thirty-five thousand miles. Ships on these routes are traveling ninety thousand miles per day, a distance equaling more than three times around the world. The one thousand two hundred and sixty-nine airports are rapidly becoming pivotal points of social progress.

In this connection we must not forget the potent influence of the telephone and the radio. Over the seventy-five million miles of telephone wire in the United States some eighty-two million calls are sent daily. Seventeen million of the twenty-eight million American homes are bound together through this means of thought exchange, while nine of the twenty-eight million feel the unifying effect of the radio.

In view of this brief survey of the mechanical instrumentalities of intercourse and understanding it is hard to believe that ever again our nation will be torn by civil strife or misunderstanding. Commercially we cannot afford it; socially we cannot tolerate it.

That which we have achieved nationally we must now seek to experience internationally. The two national problems of one hundred years ago—understanding and control—have now become world wide in scope and importance. If the philosopher and the scientist, the statesman and the engineer, supported by a generous people through legal processes and mechanical devices, could build a continental consciousness, they can now by means of the same instruments create an international mind.

The cordial exchange of greetings between President Hoover and Dieudonne Coste and Maurice Bellonte on September 8, 1930, indicates something of the trend of future international contacts. These men had succeeded in making the first non-stop flight between Paris and New York. The President's welcome and their response individualized the relationship between these countries.

"It gives me great pleasure," said he, "to welcome you here to-day. Every American recalls the thirty hours and more of intense emotion that gripped us while our own Colonel Lindbergh was winging his way to Paris, and the sense of relief and joy that swept over the nation when word came that he had safely landed. Our pride and happiness were redoubled when we heard of the magnificent reception given to him by the government and people of France. Our hearts went out in fraternal warmth to those who had so royally welcomed our national hero.

"To-day, therefore, every American knows exactly what pride and happiness possesses every French heart, at the knowledge that these two gallant sons of France stand safely on our soil. We wish the people of France to know that our welcome of their two heroes is warm and spontaneous and universal. We rejoice that this brilliant feat has been accomplished."

"Three years ago," said Coste in reply to the President, "France had the great honor of receiving and hailing two of the glories of your country— Lindbergh and Byrd. Their exploits gave to the French people the opportunity of proving to the American people the deep affection which we had fostered for more than 150 years.

"The welcome which has just been given us is a token of the reciprocal feeling of the American nation. We appreciate it to its full value and we ask you, Mr. President, to receive the homage of our deepest gratitude."

Such an event reminds us of the remarks of Victor Hugo, who, while presiding over a great conference in Paris in 1849, prophesied that:

"A day will come when those two immense groups, the United States of America and the United States of Europe, shall be seen extending the hand of fellowship across the ocean, exchanging their produce, their commerce, their industry, their arts, their genius, clearing the earth, peopling the deserts, meliorating the creation under the eye of the Creator, and uniting for the good of all, these two irresistible and infinite powers, the fraternity of men and the power of God."

President Hoover, to the pleasure of all those interested in a better world understanding, has used modern mechanical devices to a remarkable degree in his efforts to reach agreements with other countries. He has been able to humanize world problems. Treaty making has been taken out of the realm of impersonal communication and placed within the sphere of personal negotiation. We as a people were introduced to this direct contact method of approach when through the eyes of the public press we saw our President and the Prime Minister of Great Britain sitting on the side of a log in the woods of Virginia, discussing world problems. And we now dare to believe that this log will become as symbolic of international good-will in the realm of political economy as the Mark Hopkins log has of human interest in the field of education. Such visits make possible long distance communication of an intimate nature. The Peace Pact made us citizens of a legally warless world, while modern mechanical instruments of communication make us residents of a neighborly world. What then shall we say of the responsibility of the individual and of the nation in this modern world equipped with a legal and mechanical heritage and with a knowledge, we hope, of the fraternity of men and the power of God in human affairs. The answer, we believe, is to be found in the words of the late Chief Justice William Howard Taft:

"The development of the doctrine of international arbitration, considered from the standpoint of its ultimate benefits to the human race, is the most vital movement of modern times."

PUBLIC OPINION AND CONCENTRATED EFFORT

The magnitude of the problem of world peace and the far-reaching effects of its solution carries a challenge to all world minded citizens. They believe that we must now attempt to properly evaluate two social agencies—the supremacy of public opinion and the sovereignty of concentrated individual and collective effort in "the dynamic development of the forces of good will."

President Coolidge once called attention to the power of public opinion when he said:

"World peace, a world affair, stands or falls by world opinion. If we are to have world peace, in other words, we must have the necessary world opinion to support it. And, if we are to have this opinion, we must have the right feeling underneath it. Such feeling, in turn, can exist only if races and nations be convinced that aggression and exploitation have had their day, that brute force is to be brought under mental and ethical control, that all-around justice is the fixed purpose—that civilization, in short, is to establish itself conclusively over barbarism. Feeling issues in thought, thought in action.

What, therefore, could be more desirable than public expressions calculated to make international feeling what it ought to be, in order that international action may be what it ought to be?"

Enlightened individual opinion, when expressed simply, sincerely, and systematically, soon becomes public opinion. When public opinion crystallizes into national judgment it becomes effective in creating world opinion, and when world opinion resolves itself into an international code of ethics, world peace becomes a possibility.

But how shall we test the validity of the supremacy of an enlightened public opinion aroused through individual action in preventing war? Let us assume the attitude of the pragmatic philosopher and ask—will it work? Has it worked? Can individual leadership be effective on such a vast scale as that necessary in changing a world situation? Let us see.

One morning in the winter of 1924 Victor Fremont Lawson, owner and editor of the *Chicago Daily News,* during a visit with Edward Price Bell, one of his associates, sat discussing world affairs. Said Mr. Lawson to Mr. Bell, "I am thinking of Europe —apparently there is chaos material and mental. I can make no coherence of thought anywhere. Unless the leaders pull themselves together I am afraid the consequences of the war are going to be even worse than the war itself." A few days later Mr. Bell, in a letter, proposed to Mr. Lawson that an attempt be made to secure "from each of the most responsible officials of Europe a carefully reasoned statement designed to correct existing misunderstandings, allay inflammation, point the way to reconstruction and define the principles of an established international accord. It was suggested that such statements published throughout the world might prove a real service toward restoration of constructive mental processes." To this proposal Mr. Lawson gave approval without hesitation and without reservation. Arrangements were made for Mr. Bell to go to Europe immediately, for the purpose of interviewing Marx of Germany, Mussolini of Italy, Poincaré of France, and MacDonald of England. He later visited Coolidge of America, King of Canada, Wood of the Philippines, Kato of Japan, and Shao-Yi of China, together with other representatives of these countries. These men at that time were carrying many of the political responsibilities of the world, inasmuch as they were or had been the governmental leaders of their respective countries.

More than a quarter of a century before, Mr. Lawson had established a special foreign service, the purpose of which was world-wide publicity. He believed that "all nations, rightly studied, are likable." Stimulated and inspired by this belief he was willing and anxious to undertake the problem of discussing and interpreting the opinion of these world leaders and of carrying the result to people everywhere through the instrumentalities of the public press. His representatives in the various countries were known and recognized as foreign correspondents of sympathy and understanding. It was their duty to interpret international affairs in the light of twentieth century progress. Such news was to be a new feature of modern journalism.

In order for Mr. Bell to interview these national political leaders and put their statements into permanent form it was necessary for him to make a journey of nearly thirty-six thousand miles and to labor intensively for nearly two years. But he was challenged by the seriousness of the work because governmental affairs at that time both in Europe and in the Orient were, as many believed, in a chaotic condition. Shall we consider some of the statements of those men and then picture if we can, the far-reaching effect of their opinions. Shall we let Chancellor Marx of Germany speak:

"Heavy wars disarm peoples in their minds; only the abolition of the teachings of war and of the objective symbols of war can keep peoples disarmed in their minds. If we are to abolish war we must forget war. If we are to abolish war we must fill the minds and souls of our young with the gospel, the emotions and images of peace."

Then Mussolini of Italy:

"Internationalism would not be safe for a single nation; it is safe for all nations moving in concert toward a rational scheme of political, economic, and cultural intercourse. Nations need, and generally realize that they need, a lasting foundation of pacific co-existence. Such a foundation cannot be had without skillful and patient building, and such building is out of the question without established machinery for conducting international affairs in accordance with deliberately-developed world opinion. Governments and people must work together. They can work together only by understanding one another. They can understand one another only, so to speak, by foregathering in a common council chamber or forum."

And King of Canada:

"There is no reason why war should come in the Pacific; there is every reason why it should not—every reason from every angle of observation. Cultural interchange, friendly, free, continuous, progressive this, not war, is what the Orient needs, and what the Occident needs, in the Pacific. Our civilizations, in other words, are not antagonistic, not mutually exclusive but complementary. This is the great fact for statesmen and for all moral and intellectual leaders to grasp and to push powerfully to the front."

And Kato of Japan:

"To the peace of the Pacific we Japanese are devoted. We are devoted to it ardently. It never will be broken by a wanton act by Japan."

These opinions so ably and fearlessly expressed, brought confidence and cooperation to a highly irritated world. There are few, if any, greater examples of the power of aroused public thought. This effort proves that world opinion can be quickly mobilized and that once it is focused upon a problem it can be solved by discussion, agreement, and compromise, rather than by force of arms. The statements from which the foregoing excerpts were taken were appraised by President Coolidge on November 20, 1925, in the following words:

"In these carefully wrought statements of sentiment and opinion we have, I conceive, a peculiarly suggestive and important achievement in the field of international conciliation."

This work and the public expressions of opinion by these world leaders helped to pave the way for the greatest document in the history of international agreements, the Kellogg Peace Pact. Thus the supremacy of public opinion was recognized in world affairs. A few individual citizens had assumed the responsibility of leadership even though such leadership involved great personal sacrifice.

But to carry this expression of public belief and conviction into effect in a practical way, thinkers of the various races and peoples must give adequate recognition to the sovereignty of concentrated effort.

It must be clearly understood that effort may be the result of emotion on the one hand, or rational thinking on the other. To accept the former without the latter leads to radical decisions and maladjustments. To depend upon the latter without the former leads to cold, rigid, and formal action. In the future an appeal to the emotion aside from the appeal to reason will be considered in the realm of intellectual endeavor as a moral and social error, while an appeal to reason without proper appreciation of emotion will be considered in the realm of aesthetic perception as an ethical and spiritual injustice. Reliance upon both feeling and fact combined as they should be in public opinion, will guarantee well-poised, evenly balanced, judicious deliberation. When public opinion through individual interest grows to a point where a feeling knowledge of facts, processes and situations is experienced, thought mobilization takes place. People are then ready to act. The task of mobilizing thought, because of the inherent nature of the case, is an individual problem, for if an individual is to be emotionally and at the same time intellectually aroused he must in some measure understand the implications of that which compels him, as one of the many, to think. Certainly that which he thinks must have some bearing on his sense of justice, fair play or honesty, even if it does not react directly upon his own personality.

The quickness with which an individual forms unimportant judgments and makes trivial decisions, as contrasted with the deliberation with which he forms important judgments and makes weighty decisions, marks him a person of failure or achievement. So it is with nations. Based upon this type of individual and collective deliberation the sovereignty of effort finds its highest expression.

In view of this fact let us consider some tangible opportunity for individual and concentrated effort in creating a better world situation. As individuals, we shall from time to time be called upon to bear our share of the responsibility and give reasonable leadership to some of the institutions in which we hold membership. In fact, public duty will demand just this. Disraeli once said, "Individualities may form communities, but it is institutions alone that can create a nation." This statement probably was truer when Disraeli made it than it is now, on account of the almost limitless power of the individual through direct contact with people. Nevertheless much work is to be done through organizations where close personal contact is possible. This being true, in our efforts to bring about a better understanding among peoples, races or countries, through research and communication, intensive effort must be directed toward the task of changing some of the foundation principles of some of our institutions.

Good-will must be supplemented with constructive effort. It then becomes aggressive good-will, which, as we have seen, has an intellectual as well as an emotional quality. It culminates in effort that is at once strong and reasonable. This is exactly what President Hoover wants. He is concerned with what institutions do as well as with what individuals think. He is well aware of the fact that many modern organizations need to re-examine their structural framework. But in spite of the weaknesses which are easily seen by any student of social progress, President Hoover believes that the government must have the support of present-day social and spiritual institutions if it is to advance the principle of good-will.

The first of these is the church. This institution with its roots deep in the history of the past has as one of its objectives the creation of good-will in the world. Members of the church have been charged with the fulfillment of certain spiritual laws—love your enemies—do good to them that despitefully use you—whatsoever ye would that men should do to you do ye even so to them. If these laws are to become operative here and now, every effort must be made to have them function as the common law of the nation and of the world as well as of the individual. Their observance must be accepted as a human responsibility rather than as a worthy but unattainable ideal.

"Hardly anything in modern civil life," says President Hoover, "is more encouraging than the new human feeling, the deep human interest now so widespread among governments. In this devotion to human life they gladly recognize assistance and leadership of the churches, which constantly hold before their governments the ideals of courage, charity, sympathy, honor, gentleness, goodness and faith. The governments know that the life of the world cannot be saved if the soul of the world is allowed to be lost."

Too long the church has placed its moral sanction upon war as an institution. Without such sanction it could not exist. In the light of governmental action we as individual members must now individualize this national problem by taking a personal interest in it. We need to become familiar with the attitude our people have always taken and seriously consider ways and means of arousing an abiding interest in actually making our religious ideals function in a peaceful society. As voting members we may need to change our creed so as to give large place to the insistence upon a better understanding of international problems. We need, from time to time, to spiritualize friendship.

We may want to help make the symbols and images of war symbols and images of mutual understanding, for as Emerson has said, "a symbol always stimulates the intellect." Just as peace and prosperity are the rational indicators of a nation's worth, so the stimulators of a nation's thought are the symbols of peace and prosperity.

We shall of course want to help make the World Peace Pact a reality in the life of every child by keeping it properly displayed in places of worship. We shall want at all times to consider the idea of the brotherhood of man as equally important as the idea of the fatherhood of God. We shall understand that the one cannot be a reality without the other. As individuals directing the affairs of the church today we can with profit give heed to the admonition of St. Augustine in his advice to the clergy some fifteen hundred years ago.

"Thou shalt unite the citizens of one place with those of another, nation with nation, group with group, and, in general all men among themselves; and so not only render society more secure, but form a universal brotherhood."

This program calls for men and women with vision commensurate with modern needs and demands. The church ballot in their hands may become either an agency of progress or an implement of destruction. If it is to be the former we must supplant that which some writers call a religion of nationalism with an individual love of country which will produce an attitude of constructive service rather than blind sacrifice. Those who agree with Mr. Hoover that there is a spark of Divinity in every person feel that when we kill a man either legally or illegally we interfere with spiritual processes if indeed we do not disturb spiritual reality itself.

If the last decade has taught any social lesson of importance, it is that a politically warless world must be sustained in large measure by a spiritually warless church—a church of good-will. If the statesman can delegalize war, certainly the churchmen should at least attempt to despiritualize it by frankly admitting that it is contrary to its foundation principles and by substituting for it a program of helpfulness. This action in the various churches in the various countries of the world should go forward simultaneously with governmental negotiations. There is nothing radical nor impossible about it. Such a program simply creates and fosters public opinion in favor of world friendship.

If the statesmen can delegalize war, and if the churchmen can despiritualize it, perhaps it is not too much to ask that the schoolmen de-intellectualize it. This is a challenge to the modern educator, because the school has always been a unifying and socializing agency. He cannot escape this intellectual and moral responsibility. He knows that the public expects him to teach the youth of our country how to play, work and live together. As he studies history, geography and related subjects with his students he is expected to impress them with the seriousness of social responsibility. In fact he must even make some contribution to the problem of crime prevention. To this ideal he is devoted. He helps to stabilize the social order by discovering and establishing certain flexible rules of human conduct. Then war comes. Within a few months every constructive social principle which he has taught has been broken by the very government that supported his program of education. He then realizes that something needs to be done about war itself. He concludes that we cannot use it as an instrument of progress. But how can he prove it? He finds the answer within the limits of his own study.

If we turn with him to the science of biology and inquire concerning the law of physiological progress we discover a comparatively new theory of physical and social advancement. We learn, as we have already suggested, of the validity of the theory of the survival of the fittest as contrasted with the theory of differentiation of function within an organic unit of life. The former gives weight and dignity to power while the latter places stress and emphasis on variety of response. The principle of biological selection forming the idea of the survival of the fittest has given rise to the theory of social selection. This in turn has led to imperialistic autocracy. Might has been recognized as a matter of supreme achievement. It has been the object of the small as well as the great, and the weak as well as the strong. It has been considered the crowning glory of individual and social achievement. It has given us the idea of the superman.

Careful students and scholars have now come to the conclusion that the premise is false. The theory of differentiation of function within an organic unit of life has given a place of value in biological progress to every part of the living body. This theory holds that every section of the body has its work to do and its contribution to make. It also holds that every individual in a species, no matter how small or weak, has a task to perform if biological progress or growth is to take place in the group as a whole. In a word, speciety depends upon differentiation of function in the whole group rather than upon the survival power of a few of the more vigorous members of the group. This idea of differentiation has made possible and probable the application of the principle of good-will by a democratic government. Instead, then, of sacrificing the weak and the small they are conserved as vital elements in the preservation of the group to which they belong. If a condition of physical progress is variety of experience then a condition of moral or social progress is variety of virtuous response. Differentiation or variation then, has come to be recognized as the basic principle of a democracy and it naturally follows that it is also the fertile soil of social progress. But just at this point it would appear that two great schools of thought disagree. The fundamentalist in religion, the conservative in politics, the disciplinarian in education, would naturally take the side of fixed and rigid law while the modernist in religion, the progressive in politics, and the liberalist in education would plead for variety and freedom. Which side then, shall the American Individualist take? The answer is neither. In his effort to establish peaceful relationships among people and thereby guarantee human progress he will neither be rigid nor loose in his attitudes. In all of life's processes he will seek ordered variety—variety, if you will, that is the outgrowth of inherent natural law; variety the growth of which is stimulated by definite aims and purposes. Ordered variety provides opportunity for difference in form and agreement in function. It emphasizes the essentials and minimizes the nonessentials. In short, this appears to be the primary law of natural growth and it is hoped that it will become the fundamental principle of social development. With such an ideal of life we can de-intellectualize war. Democracy can succeed, and its philosophy can be applied to universal need.

Modern education has assumed this responsibility. This is true, we believe, because ordered freedom follows ordered variety as night follows day. Just as we once believed that conscience was the ultimate guide to moral action we believed that freedom was the final aim of education. Just as we now know that an educated conscience is the ultimate guide to moral conduct we now know that ordered freedom is the final aim of learning. This type of freedom gives a large place to liberty but it also lays special emphasis upon restraint. The world minded American Individualist then, will find a place in his social scheme of life for freedom of this character—the ideal of liberty will lead him along the great highway of life while the idea of restraint will prevent his turning down the bypaths that lead to misunderstanding and war.

Spencer once said that "When a man's knowledge is not in order, the more he has the greater will be his confusion of thought." And may we add that when a man's freedom is not in order the more he has the greater will be his confusion of action. The logical sequence seems to be that when a nation's freedom is not in order the more it has the greater will be its confusion of action.

From an intellectual point of view then, the will to ordered freedom is superior in individual and national affairs to the will to power and honor. The new theory of biological progress has changed our point of view in social progress. If the theory of the "survival of the fittest" is correct then perhaps we shall always have war, but if the theory of "differentiation of function" is true we must set about the task of carrying this idea to all mankind, for by so doing we rob war of one of its strongest supports.

For further support of the program to de-intellectualize war we must turn to the science of psychology because we must learn, if we can, if it is necessary to change human nature before we can stop war. This suggestion at once compels a discussion of the so-called pugnacious instinct.

If President Hoover, in his desire to act without personal bias or political prejudice upon a question which might involve war, were to make a thorough study of the cause of either personal or group conflict, he would find three well-defined and limited opinions upon this subject.

In the first place he would find people who are thoroughly convinced that there is an instinctive urge inherent in the individual that causes him to fight. Such a theory is expressed in some such sentences as these: "Fighting is an animal instinct and it is a fundamental urge in man. Before the institution of war can be abolished this instinctive tendency must be eliminated if possible through the ordinary processes of physical evolution. If it cannot be destroyed through the growth of the race war cannot be stopped. Accordingly we cannot hope for a cessation of war within the near future. It may even be centuries before the world can expect international peace." This psychological theory is closely related to the religious doctrine of predestination once held by a considerable group of conscientious people. But just as the educator showed the false assumption of this religious tenet by advancing the theory of the improvability of man through education, the scientist now disproves this psychological doctrine by declaring that his researches do not support a belief in a deterministic universe. People who accept the instinctive urge to fight as one of the basic human controls, in spite of all the evidence to the contrary, seem to be satisfied with society as it is. They take it for granted that since there has always been war there always will be war.

In the second place he would find those who believe that "we must admit that brutal instincts are an inheritance, the existence of which we cannot escape, but that we are apt to forget that the actions in which these instincts find expression are within man's control." Supporters of this theory naturally conclude that the fighting instinct "should not in the national scale lead to warfare any more than they lead on the individual scale normally to murder or duelling." This theory gives education a large place in the program of creating a friendly social order. The success of the individual under these conditions depends upon his ability to push into the background of his life the inherent or fundamental urges which are both antagonistic and destructive, while he gives the higher and nobler drives opportunity of expression. With this Mr. Hoover agrees. He says that "The problem of the world is to restrain the destructive instincts while strengthening and enlarging those of altruistic character and constructive impulse—for thus we build for the future." Under these conditions a person must constantly struggle against the anti-social responses which he feels tempted to make. His life is one of conflict between the so-called primary urges and action habits. While the individual might feel reasonably secure under these circumstances, particularly when his habits became definitely fixed, society always faces the possibility of unexpected outbreaks. This is true because custom cannot have the same restraining power of control in the group that habit has in the individual. War under these conditions would always be a possibility.

In the third place he would find another school of modern thinkers who deny the existence of a fighting instinct. As a matter of fact these scholars do not find sufficient evidence to warrant belief in any of the so-called human instincts, especially when they are considered as inborn drives. Life is too plastic and free to be either directed or controlled by such rigid determiners. Human action which was formerly thought to be the result of instinctive urges is now believed to be the outgrowth of organic sensations or learned habits of response.

Anyone at all familiar with the complex structure and function of the nervous system of the child knows that there is no set of fixed drives or responses such as the behavior pattern found in the insect or even in the bird. Some of the lower forms of life are almost completely developed when they come into the world. Their nervous system is ready at once to function effectively. This is not so with man. He is by no means a finished product at the time of his birth. His capacity for growth and adaptation is very great for he is not controlled by predetermined psychological entities.

In view of these facts we need to re-examine our social philosophy in order to be able to give direction to our governmental activities. If there is no fighting instinct in man, there is no reason why we should keep the world organized for war, because we are not acting contrary to human nature if we dwell peaceably on the earth. More than that, we do not have to change human nature in order to stop war. All we need to do is to change a social and national custom. This is not beyond the limits of human possibility. Indeed it should not be as hard to change social custom as it is a personal habit. Custom may sometimes lie buried deep in the soil of mental and economic action, but habit may be rooted in the physical structure of the body itself.

President Hoover is right, then, when he says that the more complex the problems of the Nation become, the greater is the need for more and more advanced instruction, and when he observes that:

"The foundations of American public opinion in the next generation are now being laid in the universities and colleges of the land. It is of high importance that they be laid in a spirit of international reconciliation and tolerance."

Educators now have sufficient knowledge to prove the utter futility of war. Their task is that of carrying this knowledge to the ends of the earth in order that all nations might follow the leadership of their statesmen in their efforts to make the World Peace Pact an effective instrument in maintaining international good-will.

Along by the side of the church and the school the theater stands in modern society as an institution wherein public opinion in support of a new world order is being mobilized. It has become a community center where great numbers of people gather for information, instruction, and entertainment. It is here that appeals are made to the feeling as well as to the intellect. Opinions accepted by the group are enriched by emotional response. A willingness to make some individual effort to change wrong customs is aroused. Personal responsibility is assumed. If for instance a person somewhat doubtful of the possibility of "the dynamic development of the forces of good-will" would attend a theater where "All Quiet on the Western Front" is being shown, his faith in the promotion of international understanding would be increased. He would share the evening's entertainment with an audience serious in attitude and restrained in emotional response. He would notice that both old and young readily catch the spirit of the warrior as he jests and jokes. But at the same time he would know that they sense the gravity and seriousness of the entire business in which the soldier is engaged. He would learn that it is easier for them to weep during periods of serious portrayal than it is to laugh during times of jovial and social discussion. At only one point does the audience applaud. It is at a time when common sense expressed in homely philosophic terms gains recognition over all that is trivial on the one hand or idealistic on the other. Sitting on the sunny side of a hut reviewing the fortunes of war, the main characters of the story fall into a discussion and even an argument concerning the responsibility of the com-

mon people. One argues that "if all had the same
grub and the same pay, the war would be over and
done in a day," while another suggests that "a declaration of war should be a kind of popular festival
with entrance tickets and bands like a bull fight and
then in the arena the ministers and generals of the
two countries dressed in bathing drawers and armed
with clubs, can have it out among themselves. Who-
ever survives, his country wins. That would be much
simpler and more just than this arrangement where
the wrong people do the fighting."

Of course the picture, together with the spoken
words, touches the imagination of the average person and the reasonableness of the suggestion at once
calls for expression, which in turn becomes almost
unanimous as the audience approves. Even a casual
observer readily recognizes that the common people
do not wage war. They neither want it nor start it
even though they fight it. The theater is bringing
this consideration to the forefront of national
thought. It uses as its agencies in creating favorable
public opinion the three-fold instrument—the written message, the moving picture and the spoken
word. For more than a quarter of a century the
moving picture has not only fired the imagination but
provided a vicarious experience which laid the foundation for sound and reasonable judgment on the
part of the public. It has been supported and sustained by the printed word and made living and
realistic as it is thrown on the screen by the powerful projecting machine. For more than three hun-

dred years the printed page has served as a means of communication between the teacher and those taught, the leader and those led, the commander and those commanded. But now for the first time in human history the average citizen of our country can read a book, see it interpreted on the screen, and hear spoken the very words used by the author. Through this three-fold method of interpretation a series of facts become indelibly outlined in individual thought and finally take form in definite principles which may eventually become the ideals of a nation. Because of it war can no longer be considered by people of a succeeding generation as merely an institution. It used to create one state of mind while it was in progress, but another after it was over. Following generations too often considered only the glories of it all. They thought in abstract terms about it. But now the talking picture reduces it to physical and material terms. We can see and even hear it. We experience it vicariously. In times past we have believed that if the dead could speak there would be no more war. In a way they do speak in pictures. They make real its horror. The talking picture makes war a human problem. It singles out people. It strikes at the very center of society. It kills individuals.

President Hoover then, has supporting his program of world peace instruments of communication more impressive and powerful than those used by any of his predecessors. Having assumed the authority and responsibility involved in executing his duties as the president of a nation which has approved the World Peace Pact, he has made bold his peace program because of the government's ability to reach not only the intellect, but the emotions of the people.

Supplementing the work of these popular agencies the governmental leader today finds another type of organization at work in human society, having as one of their major purposes that of creating international good will. Notable among these are the various Women's clubs and Rotary International. These two organizations alone have within their membership the understanding, vision and influence to make the present world ideal become a reality. Mr. Hoover, in appointing President Mary Emma Woolley as a delegate to the Geneva Conference on the reduction of arms took occasion to recognize this interest by saying: "The whole question of disarmament is, and has been, of profound interest to the women of the United States. They have shown this interest in it for many years and I have determined to appoint a prominent woman as a member of the delegation."

In speaking to an audience of representative business men of the world, meeting under the auspices of the International Chamber of Commerce in Washington on May 4, 1931, he said: "The United States has a less direct interest in land armament reduction than any of the large nations because our forces have been already demobilized and reduced more than all others. We have, however, a vast indirect interest in greater assurance of peace, order and the increased economic prosperity of other nations. It is within the power of business men of the world to insist that this problem shall be met with sincerity, courage and constructive action."

Rotarians who are at the same time filling places of leadership in other national and international associations have been among the first men of the world to appreciate the facts involved in the President's words. They have impressed the importance of their Sixth Object upon the world through a program of local, national, and world fellowship. They support our government in "the advancement of understanding, goodwill and international peace through a world fellowship of business and professional men united in the ideal of service."

COOPERATIVE INDIVIDUALISM

All of these spiritual and educational considerations substantiate Mr. Hoover's philosophy of good will and favor the development of the theory of cooperative individualism as the best means to its attainment. For centuries governmental executives believed that a satisfactory social structure could be built by sacrificing the individual for the good of the group or the minority for the good of the majority. This theory of political control was not opposed by the people so long as they believed that social advancement was achieved mainly through the acquisition and use of things, property, and even people themselves. But if hundreds of years of human experience has taught a single truth of value for this generation it is the fact that social progress comes not through accumulation but through growth because both science and sociology support the conclusion that individual advancement occurs simultaneously with physical, mental and moral development. This fact supports President Hoover in his contentions that progress must come from "the steady lift of the individual and that the measure of national idealism and progress is the quality of idealism in the individual."

Now if the thesis of this chapter is correct, namely that war is the greatest obstacle to our American individualistic way of life because it permits and often demands that government officials enter the domain of the private citizen and curtail his initiative, limit his opportunity, and thereby destroy his liberty, it becomes the duty of the government to find ways and means of eliminating it as an instrument of control. If, on the other hand, the development of a spirit of good will throughout the world is the means by which the institution of war can be abolished, it becomes the individual's and the nation's greatest asset. Throughout these pages we have tried to show that it is the most essential quality of the person who believes in the theory of American Individualism. This being true, it seems reasonable that the power of good will must rapidly supplant the force of arms as an agency of local, national, and world security. As good will rises in the scale of human values to the level where it embraces international amity, the use of force will decrease to the point where it will be needed only for world wide police protection. Within the history of our country the limits of the social safety zone of the individual has been extended at least three times—in the small group—later in the nation, and now in the world.

During the period preceding the establishment of our national government, small groups or colonies of people entered into agreements with each other for the specific purpose of making society safe for the individual. The necessity for the maintenance of this policy continued up to and in some cases after the adoption of the National Constitution. For instance, hundreds of treaties have been made between our federal government and Indian tribes. Many of these treaties were authorized in order to guarantee security to the individual citizen within the boundaries of a comparatively small territory and within the limits of a small circle of people. During this period one of the most important problems of society was that of providing safety for all through the development of the ideal of fraternalistic individualism.

The second period of expansion had its beginning at the time of the adoption of the National Constitution when the states set up a federal government. At that time, or certainly by 1791 when the first ten amendments were adopted, the national government began to assume some responsibility for the individual's rights and safety. While the ideal of this document involved the desire on the part of the government to organize a nation without factional disturbances and without sectional strife, it could not be realized instantaneously, but just at the time when the theory of a united nation was accepted by the people of our country the safety of the individual citizen within its boundaries became assured. Since that indeterminable moment in American history we have developed a spirit of national loyalty to which we give expression in the following declaration: "We pledge allegiance to the flag of the United States of America and to the republic for which it stands, one nation indivisible, with liberty and justice for all." Under the commanding inspiration of citizenship in an indivisible nation, fraternalistic individualism now becomes nationalistic individualism.

Since the World War we have definitely entered the third stage of expansion because we have discovered that so long as there is a possibility of war between nations the individual in no nation is secure. The loss of more than seven and one-half million men representing various nations in the World War, taught the tragic truth of this observation. Since then governmental officials have recognized the fact and have signed the World Peace Pact, the aim of which, in the final analysis is to make the world safe for the individual. President Hoover, in surveying present international conditions, finds that through it "a great moral standard has been raised in the world."

This international moral standard will shape national ideals and these ideals will encourage the development of a spirit of individual helpfulness and a willingness to assume social obligation universal in nature. Indeed the central theme of the President's philosophy of Individualism assumes that the world cannot be made secure without the assumption of individual responsibility commensurate with the privileges enjoyed. He well knows that this rhythmical interaction between the individual and the people of the world through the agencies of our national government for the peaceful settlement of controversies, including the World Court, will extend the boundaries of the realm of personal security and make possible the development of a philosophy of internationalistic individualism, all of which rests on the foundation of the intrinsic value and common sense of the common man.

QUOTATIONS

INDEX

253